D1572533

✠

The Ancient Faith Prayer Book

Compiled and edited by

VASSILIOS PAPAVASSILIOU

ANCIENT FAITH
PUBLISHING

CHESTERTON, INDIANA

The Ancient Faith Prayer Book

Compilation copyright ©2014 by Ancient Faith Publishing

Published by:
    Ancient Faith Publishing
    A Division of Ancient Faith Ministries
    P.O. Box 748
    Chesterton, IN 46304

ISBN: 9781936270-90-3

Printed in the United States of America

CONTENTS

How to Use This Book   5

1   Morning Prayers   7

2   Afternoon Prayers   25

3   Prayers for Mealtimes   35

4   Early Evening Prayers   41

5   Late Evening Prayers   51

6   Canon for Holy Communion   67

7   Prayers Before Holy Communion   77

8   Thanksgiving After Holy Communion   97

9   Prayers for the Departed   109

10   Prayers for Confession   113

11   Prayers for Various Needs and Occasions   119

12   Prayers of the Saints   139

Calendar of Great Feasts and Fasts   168

Do not concern yourself with the number of prayers read, but only lift your heart and mind to the Lord in prayer, and continue in a worthy manner for the time set aside.

A few prayers, correctly read, are better than many prayers raced through. And, of course, it is hard to keep from rushing when, in our eagerness to pray, we have gathered more prayers than we can handle.

—St. Theophan the Recluse

HESE WORDS OF St. Theophan— undoubtedly one of the greatest teachers of prayer the Orthodox Church has ever produced—were the inspiration for the "rule of prayer" followed in this book: a rule made to be broken. You hold in your hands a rich collection of prayers for set times of day taken from the Book of Hours (the *Horologion*), representing the ancient tradition of Orthodox devotion, as well as prayers for various needs and occasions and prayers composed by numerous saints of the Church from East and West. But no one should feel obliged to say them all. This prayer book offers variety and flexibility according to each person's situation and capability. For this reason, in the "set" prayers found in these pages, choices of one or more psalms and prayers are given. The focus of one's *prayer rule* (often suggested by one's spiritual father) should not be the *rule*, but the *prayer*. Therefore, let the attention be not on the "one" or the "all," but on learning to pray "in spirit and truth" (John 4:24).

N THE NAME of the Father and of the Son and of the Holy Spirit. AMEN.

O Heavenly King, Comforter, Spirit of Truth, everywhere present and filling all things, Treasury of blessings and Giver of life, come and abide in us, cleanse us from every stain, and save our souls, O Good One.

*If it is the Paschal season, the above prayer
is replaced by the apolytikion of Pascha:*

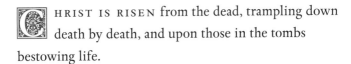 HRIST IS RISEN from the dead, trampling down death by death, and upon those in the tombs bestowing life.

THE TRISAGION PRAYERS

 OLY GOD, Holy Mighty, Holy Immortal One, have mercy on us. *(3x)*

Glory to the Father and to the Son and to the Holy Spirit, both now and forever and to the ages of ages. AMEN.

O Most Holy Trinity, have mercy on us. O Lord, cleanse us from our sins. O Master, pardon our iniquities. O Holy One, visit and heal our infirmities for Your name's sake.

Lord, have mercy. *(3x)*

Glory to the Father and to the Son and to the Holy Spirit, both now and forever and to the ages of ages. AMEN.

Our Father in heaven, hallowed be Your name. Your kingdom come; Your will be done on earth as it is in heaven. Give us this day our daily bread. And forgive us our trespasses as we forgive those who trespass against us. And lead us not into temptation, but deliver us from the evil one.

Lord, have mercy. *(12x)*

Come, let us worship God our King.

Come, let us worship and fall down before Christ, our
King and our God.

Come, let us worship and fall down before Christ
Himself, our King and our God.

A Prayer of Thanksgiving

AVING RISEN FROM SLEEP, I thank You,
O Holy Trinity, because through Your great goodness and longsuffering You have not been angry with
me, an idler and a sinner, nor have You destroyed me
in my iniquities. But rather You have shown me Your
customary love for mankind and roused me, as I lay
in despair, to rise in the morning and to glorify Your
might. And now, enlighten the eyes of my mind and
open my mouth to meditate on Your words, to understand Your commandments, and to do Your will, to sing
to You with confession of heart, and to praise Your all-
holy name, of the Father and of the Son and of the Holy
Spirit, now and forever, and to the ages of ages. AMEN.

Prayer of St. Philaret of Moscow

Lord, grant me to greet the coming day in peace. Help me in all things to rely upon Your holy will. In every hour of the day, reveal Your will to me. Bless my dealings with all who surround me. Teach me to treat all that comes to me throughout the day with peace of soul and with the firm conviction that Your will governs all. In all my deeds and words, guide my thoughts and feelings. In unforeseen events, let me not forget that all are sent by You. Teach me to act firmly and wisely, without embittering and embarrassing others. Give me strength to bear the fatigue of the coming day with all that it shall bring. Direct my will; teach me to pray; pray You Yourself in me. Amen.

Then we may say one or all of the following psalms:

PSALM 120

I have lifted up my eyes to the mountains, whence my help will come.
My help is from the Lord, who made heaven and earth.
Let not your foot waver, and He who guards you will not slumber.

Behold, He who guards Israel will neither slumber nor sleep.

The Lord will protect you; the Lord will shield you with His
*   right hand.*

The sun will not scorch you by day, nor the moon by night.

The Lord will defend you against every evil;
*   the Lord will protect your soul.*

The Lord will guard your coming and going, now and
*   forevermore.*

PSALM 89

O Lord, You have been our refuge from generation to
*   generation.*

You were there before the mountains came to be and the earth
*   and the world were formed. You are from everlasting to*
*   everlasting.*

Turn not man unto lowliness. For You said, "Return to Me,
*   O sons of men."*

For a thousand years in Your eyes, O Lord, are but as
*   yesterday when it is past, and as a watch in the night.*

Their years shall be of no account; in the morning like grass
*   shall they pass away; in the morning shall they blossom*
*   and fade.*

In the evening shall they fall; they shall dry up and wither.

For in Your wrath have we perished, and in Your anger have
*   we been troubled.*

You have set our iniquities before us; our years are in the light
of Your countenance.
For all our days have faded away, and in Your wrath do we
wither; our years have, like a spider, spun out their tale.
Seventy years is the span of our life, or eighty if we have
strength; and the greater number of them is toil and travail.
For meekness has come upon us, and we shall be chastened.
Who knows the might of Your wrath? And in the fear of You,
who can recount Your anger?
So make Your right hand known to me and to them that in
their heart are instructed in wisdom.
Return, O Lord; how long? Be entreated by Your servants.
We were filled in the morning with Your mercy, O Lord,
and we rejoiced and were glad.
In all our days, let us be glad for the days wherein You humbled
us, for the years wherein we saw evil things.
Look upon Your servants, and upon Your works,
and guide their sons.
Let the brightness of the Lord our God be upon us,
and direct the works of our hands to do good.
Guide the works of our hands.

PSALM 50

Have mercy on me, O God, according to Your great mercy,
and according to the greatness of Your compassion blot out
my offense.

Wash me thoroughly of my iniquity and cleanse me of my sin.
For I know my iniquity, and my sin is ever before me.
Against You alone have I sinned and done evil in Your sight,
    that You may be justified in Your words and prevail when
    You are judged.
For lo, in iniquity I was conceived, and in sins my mother
    bore me.
For lo, You have loved truth: the hidden and secret lore of
    Your wisdom have You revealed to me.
You will sprinkle me with hyssop, and I shall be cleansed;
    You will wash me, and I shall be made whiter than snow.
You will make me hear of joy and gladness; the bones which
    have been humbled will rejoice.
Turn away Your face from my sins, and blot out all my
    iniquities.
Create a clean heart in me, O God, and renew a right spirit
    within me.
Cast me not away from Your presence, and do not take Your
    Holy Spirit from me.
Restore to me the joy of Your salvation, and with Your
    sovereign Spirit establish me.
I will teach transgressors Your ways, and sinners will turn to
    You again.
Deliver me from bloodshed, O God, the God of my salvation,
    and my tongue will rejoice at Your justice.
Lord, You will open my lips, and my mouth will proclaim
    Your praise.

For if You had desired sacrifice, I would have given it; You will
not take pleasure in burnt offerings.

A sacrifice to God is a broken spirit; a broken and a humbled
heart God will not despise.

Do good to Zion, O Lord, in Your good pleasure; and let the
walls of Jerusalem be built.

Then will You be well-pleased with a sacrifice of righteousness,
with oblations and burnt offerings.

Then will they offer calves upon Your altar.

*If we are to take Communion, we may add, or instead say,
one or all of the psalms before Holy Communion
(page 77).*

THE CREED

I BELIEVE IN ONE GOD, Father Almighty,
Maker of heaven and earth and of all things visible and invisible.

And in one Lord Jesus Christ, the Only-begotten Son of
God, begotten of the Father before all ages.

Light from Light, true God from true God, begotten not
created, of one essence with the Father; through Him all
things were made.

For us men and for our salvation He came down from heaven and was incarnate of the Holy Spirit and the Virgin Mary and became man;

He was crucified also for us under Pontius Pilate, and suffered and was buried;

He rose again on the third day, in accordance with the Scriptures, and ascended into heaven, and is seated at the right hand of the Father;

He is coming again in glory to judge the living and the dead; and His kingdom will have no end.

And in the Holy Spirit, the Lord, the Giver of life, who proceeds from the Father, who together with the Father and the Son is worshipped and glorified; who spoke through the Prophets.

In one, Holy, Catholic and Apostolic Church;

I confess one Baptism for the forgiveness of sins;

I expect the resurrection of the dead and the life of the age to come. AMEN.

Morning Doxology

G LORY TO YOU who have shown us the light. Glory to God in the highest, peace on earth, and goodwill among men. We praise You, we bless You, we worship You, we glorify You, we give You thanks for Your great glory: Lord, King, God of heaven, Father Almighty; Only-begotten Son, Lord Jesus Christ; and Holy Spirit. Lord God, Lamb of God, Son of the Father, who take away the sin of the world, have mercy on us, You who take away the sins of the world. Receive our prayer, O You who sit at the right hand of the Father, and have mercy on us. For You alone are holy, You alone are Lord, Jesus Christ, to the glory of God the Father. AMEN.

Every morning will I bless You and praise Your name forever and to the ages of ages. You have been our refuge, O Lord, from generation to generation. I said, "Lord, have mercy on me, heal my soul, for against You have I sinned." To You have I fled for refuge; teach me to do Your will, for You are my God. For with You is the source of life, and in Your light shall we see light. Let Your mercy remain upon those who know You.

Lord, grant that this day we may be kept without sin. Blessed are You, O Lord, the God of our fathers, and praised and glorified is Your name forevermore. AMEN.

May Your mercy, O Lord, be upon us, for in You have we put our trust. Blessed are You, O Lord; teach me Your statutes. Blessed are You, O Master; make me understand Your statutes. Blessed are You, O Holy One; enlighten me with Your statutes. Lord, Your mercy endures forever: despise not the works of Your hands. To You is due praise, to You is due song, to You is due glory, to the Father and to the Son and to the Holy Spirit, now and forever, and to the ages of ages. AMEN.

Then we may say one or all of the following prayers from the Hours:

A PRAYER FOR 6:00 A.M.

ETERNAL GOD, the beginningless and ever-lasting Light, fashioner of all creation, fountain of mercy, abyss of goodness, and unsearchable depth of love for man: cause the light of Your countenance to shine upon us, O Lord. Shine in our hearts, O spiritual Sun of Righteousness; fill our souls with Your joy; teach us ever to ponder and proclaim Your judgments and always to give thanks to You, our Master and Benefactor. Direct the works of our hands to do Your will; guide us to do those things that are pleasing and dear to You, that through us, unworthy though we are, Your all-holy name may be glorified, of the Father and of the Son and of the Holy Spirit, one Godhead and Kingdom, to whom is due all glory, honor, and worship forever. AMEN.

ANOTHER PRAYER FOR 6:00 A.M.

YOU SEND FORTH THE LIGHT, and it goes. You make the sun to rise upon the just and the unjust, upon the evil and the good. You make the morning and give light to the whole world. Enlighten also our hearts, O Master of all. Grant that this day we may be acceptable to You; preserve us from all sin and every wicked deed; deliver us from every arrow of temptation that flies by day and from every adverse power, by the intercessions of our all-pure Lady the Mother of God, of Your bodiless ministers and heavenly hosts, and of all the saints, who have been well-pleasing to You throughout the ages. For Your will it is to have mercy and to save us, O God, and to You do we give glory, to the Father and to the Son and to the Holy Spirit, now and forever, and to the ages of ages. Amen.

A Prayer for 9:00 a.m.

Lord our God, You gave Your peace to men and sent down the gift of Your All-holy Spirit upon Your disciples and apostles, and by Your power You opened their lips with tongues of fire. Open also my lips and teach me, sinner though I am, how and for what I should pray. Guide my life, O calm Haven of the storm-tossed, and reveal the way in which I should walk. Renew a right spirit within me, and with Your Sovereign Spirit steady my mind, that, guided and guarded each day by Your good Spirit, I may be able to practice Your commandments, always remembering Your glorious presence that looks upon the deeds of men. Let me not be deceived by the corrupting delights of this world, but rather strengthen in me the desire to attain the treasures of the world to come. For blessed and praised are You in all Your saints forever and ever. Amen.

A Prayer for Every Hour

T EVERY TIME AND AT EVERY HOUR in heaven and on earth You are worshipped and glorified, O Christ our God, You who are longsuffering, most merciful, most compassionate, who love the just and are merciful to sinners, who call all to salvation through the promise of the good things to come. Accept, O Lord, our entreaties at this hour and guide our lives that we may keep Your commandments. Sanctify our souls, purify our bodies, correct our thoughts, purify our ideas, and deliver us from all distress, evil, and pain. Surround us with Your holy angels that, protected and guided by their host, we may attain unity of faith and the knowledge of Your unapproachable glory. For blessed are You forever and ever. AMEN.

If we are to take Communion, we may add, or instead say, one or all of the prayers before Holy Communion (page 77).

Lord, have mercy. *(3x)*

Glory to the Father and to the Son and to the Holy Spirit, both now and forever, and to the ages of ages. AMEN.

A Prayer to the Mother of God

GREATER IN HONOR than the cherubim, and beyond compare more glorious than the seraphim, undefiled you gave birth to God the Word: truly the Mother of God, we magnify you.

Here we may say the apolytikion of our patron saint or the following prayer:

A Prayer to our Patron Saint

PRAY TO GOD FOR ME, O Holy *(name)*, well-pleasing to God: for I turn to you, who are my swift helper and the intercessor for my soul.

A Prayer to our Guardian Angel

ANGEL OF CHRIST, holy guardian and protector of my soul and body, forgive me everything wherein I have offended you every day of my life, and protect me from all influence and temptation of the evil one. May I nevermore anger God by any sin. Pray for me to the Lord, that He may make me worthy of the grace of the All-holy Trinity, of the most-holy Mother of God, and of all the saints.

A Prayer to God for Guidance

GUIDE MY STEPS according to Your word, and let no iniquity hold sway over me. Deliver me from the slander of men, and I shall keep Your commandments. Cause Your countenance to shine upon Your servant, and teach me Your statutes. Let my mouth be filled with Your praise, O Lord, that I may sing Your glory and splendor all day long.

A Prayer to Christ for Guidance and Illumination

CHRIST, THE TRUE LIGHT, You enlighten and sanctify every man who comes into the world. Make the light of Your countenance shine upon us, that in it we may see Your unapproachable light, and guide our steps that we may keep Your commandments. By the intercessions of Your most pure Mother and of all Your saints. AMEN.

During Great Lent and Holy Week, we add the
PRAYER OF ST. EPHREM THE SYRIAN:

LORD AND MASTER OF MY LIFE, give me not a spirit of sloth, idle curiosity, love of power, and useless chatter. Rather, accord to me, Your servant, a spirit of chastity, humility, patience, and love. Yes, Lord and King, grant that I may see my own faults and not condemn my brother, for blessed are You forever and ever. AMEN.

THROUGH THE PRAYERS of our holy Fathers, Lord Jesus Christ our God, have mercy on us and save us. AMEN.

N THE NAME of the Father and of the Son and of the Holy Spirit. AMEN.

THE TRISAGION PRAYERS

 OLY GOD, Holy Mighty, Holy Immortal One, have mercy on us. *(3x)*

Glory to the Father and to the Son and to the Holy Spirit, both now and forever and to the ages of ages. AMEN.

O Most Holy Trinity, have mercy on us. O Lord, cleanse us from our sins. O Master, pardon our iniquities. O Holy One, visit and heal our infirmities for Your name's sake.

Lord, have mercy. *(3x)*

Glory to the Father and to the Son and to the Holy Spirit, both now and forever and to the ages of ages. AMEN.

Our Father in heaven, hallowed be Your name. Your kingdom come; Your will be done on earth as it is in heaven. Give us this day our daily bread. And forgive us our trespasses as we forgive those who trespass against us. And lead us not into temptation, but deliver us from the evil one.

Lord, have mercy. (*12x*)

Then we may say one or all of the following psalms:

PSALM 90

He who dwells in the help of the Most High shall dwell in the shelter of the God of heaven.

He will say to the Lord: You are my protector and my refuge, my God; in Him will I hope.

For He will deliver you from the snare of hunters and from troubling words.

With His arm will He overshadow you, and beneath His wings will you hope; as a shield will His truth encompass you.

You will fear no terror by night, nor any arrow that flies by day; no creature that moves in the darkness, nor any mishap or noonday demon.

Though a thousand fall at your side, and ten thousand at your right, yet it shall not come near you.

With your eyes you will behold and see the reward of sinners.

For You, O Lord, are my hope; You made the Most High
  Your refuge.
No evil shall befall you, nor shall any affliction approach your
  habitation.
For He has commanded His angels concerning you, to guard
  you in all your ways.
In their hands shall they bear you up, lest you dash your foot
  against a stone.
You will tread upon the asp and the basilisk, and trample the
  lion and the dragon.
Because he hoped in Me, I shall deliver him; I will shelter him,
  because he knew My name.
He will cry to Me, and I shall hear him; I am with him when
  trouble is near.
I shall deliver him and glorify him.
With long life shall I satisfy him, and show him My salvation.

PSALM 84

O Lord, You were pleased with Your land; You turned away
  the captivity of Jacob.
You forgave Your people their iniquities; You covered all
  their sins.
You made Your anger cease; You turned away from the rage of
  Your wrath.
Turn us back again, O God of our salvation, and turn away
  Your anger from us.

Will You be angry with us forever? Or will You prolong Your
    wrath from generation to generation?
O God, when You have turned us back You will quicken us,
    and Your people will rejoice in You.
Lord, show us Your mercy and grant us Your salvation.
I will hear what the Lord God will say in me; for He will utter
    words of peace to His people, to His holy ones, to those who
    turn their hearts to Him.
But His salvation is near to those who fear Him, that glory
    may dwell in our land.
Mercy and truth have met, righteousness and peace have kissed
    each other.
Truth has arisen from the earth, and righteousness has come
    down from heaven.
For the Lord will offer goodness, and our earth will bear fruit.
Righteousness shall go before Him, and His steps shall He set
    for our way.

PSALM 85

Incline Your ear, O Lord, and hear me, for I am poor
    and needy.
Guard my soul, for I am holy; O my God, save Your servant,
    for in You I hope.
Have mercy on me, O Lord, for I shall cry to You all day long;
    give joy to the soul of Your servant, for to You have I lifted
    up my soul.

*For You, O Lord, are good and gentle, and abundantly
    merciful to all who call upon You.*

*Heed my prayer, O Lord, and hear the voice of my
    supplication.*

*In the day of my affliction I called to You, for You have
    heard me.*

*There is none like You among gods, O Lord; none whose works
    are like Your works.*

*The Gentiles You created shall come and kneel before You,
    O Lord, and they shall glorify Your name.*

For You are great and do wondrous things; You alone are God.

*Guide me, O Lord, in Your way, and I shall walk in Your
    truth; make my heart glad to fear Your name.*

*With all my heart shall I give You thanks, O Lord my God;
    and I shall glorify Your name forever.*

*For great is Your mercy toward me, and from the depths of hell
    have You delivered my soul.*

*O God, lawless men rose up against me, and an assembly of
    mighty ones sought my soul, and they did not set You
    before them.*

*But You, O Lord, are compassionate and merciful, long-
    suffering, full of pity and truth.*

*Look upon me and have mercy on me; grant strength to Your
    servant and save the son of Your maidservant.*

*Give me a sign of Your goodness, and let those who hate me see
    it and be ashamed; for You, O Lord, have helped me and
    comforted me.*

GLORY TO THE FATHER and to the Son and to the Holy Spirit, both now and forever, and to the ages of ages. AMEN.

*Then we may say one or all of the following
prayers of the Hours:*

A PRAYER FOR THE NOON HOUR

GOD AND LORD OF POWERS, Maker of all creation, through the compassion of Your unfathomable mercy You sent down Your Only-begotten Son, our Lord and Savior, Jesus Christ, for the salvation of our race, and through His precious Cross tore up the record of our sins, and by it triumphed over the principalities and powers of darkness. Do You Yourself, O Master and Lover of mankind, accept also our supplications of thanksgiving and entreaty, and deliver us from transgressions of destruction and darkness, and from all our enemies, seen and unseen, who seek to harm us. Nail down our flesh through fear of You; let not our hearts be inclined to words or thoughts of evil, but wound our souls with longing for You, that ever gazing upon You and guided by the light that comes from You, we may behold Your unapproachable and everlasting light, and give thanks to You, the Eternal Father, with Your Only-begotten Son and Your All-holy, Good, and Life-giving Spirit, now and forever, and to the ages of ages. AMEN.

A PRAYER FOR 3:00 P.M.

 MASTER, LORD JESUS CHRIST our God, who have long endured our transgressions and brought us to this hour, in which, hanging on the life-giving tree, You showed the good thief the way to Paradise and destroyed death by death: have mercy also on us sinners and Your unworthy servants. For we have sinned and trespassed and are not worthy to raise our eyes and look upon the heights of heaven, because we have forsaken Your righteous ways and have followed the will of our hearts. But we implore Your unbounded goodness: spare us, O Lord, according to the greatness of Your mercy; for the sake of Your holy name, save us; for our days have been wasted in vanity. Deliver us from the hand of our enemy, forgive us our sins, and slay the will of our flesh, so that, having cast off the old man, we may put on the new and live for You, our Master and Benefactor. Thus following Your precepts may we find eternal rest, where those who rejoice abide. For

You are the true joy and gladness of those who love You, O Christ our God, and to You we give glory, together with Your Eternal Father, and Your All-holy, Good, and Life-giving Spirit, now and forever, and to ages of ages. Amen.

A Prayer for Every Hour

At every time and at every hour in heaven and on earth You are worshipped and glorified, O Christ our God, You who are longsuffering, most merciful, most compassionate, who love the just and are merciful to sinners, who call all to salvation through the promise of the good things to come. Accept, O Lord, our entreaties at this hour, and guide our lives that we may keep Your commandments. Sanctify our souls, purify our bodies, correct our thoughts, purify our ideas, and deliver us from all distress, evil, and pain. Surround us with Your holy angels that, protected and guided by their host, we may attain unity of faith and the knowledge of Your unapproachable glory. For blessed are You forever and ever. Amen.

LORD AND MASTER OF MY LIFE, give me not a spirit of sloth, idle curiosity, love of power, and useless chatter. Rather, accord to me Your servant a spirit of chastity, humility, patience, and love. Yes, Lord and King, grant that I may see my own faults and not condemn my brother, for blessed are You forever and ever. AMEN.

THROUGH THE PRAYERS of our holy fathers, Lord Jesus Christ our God, have mercy on us and save us. AMEN.

Prayer and Blessing
Before Breakfast

T HE RICH have been sent away poor and hungry, while those who seek the Lord will not be deprived of any good thing.

Glory to the Father and to the Son and to the Holy Spirit, both now and forever, and to the ages of ages. Amen.

Lord, have mercy. *(3x)*

O Christ our God, bless the food and drink of Your servants, for You are holy always, now and forever, and to the ages of ages. Amen.

Prayer After Breakfast

M AY THE LORD KEEP US all by His grace and love for mankind, always, now and forever, and to the ages of ages. Amen.

35

Prayer and Blessing
Before the Midday Meal

HE RICH have been sent away poor and hungry, while those who seek the Lord will not be deprived of any good thing.

Glory to the Father and to the Son and to the Holy Spirit, both now and forever and to the ages of ages. AMEN.

Lord, have mercy. *(3x)*

O Christ our God, bless the food and drink of Your servants, for You are holy, always, now and forever, and to the ages of ages. AMEN.

Another Blessing Before the Midday Meal

LORD JESUS CHRIST OUR GOD, who blessed the five loaves in the wilderness and from them fed five thousand, bless these gifts also, and multiply them in this household and for all Your world, and sanctify Your faithful servants who partake of them. For You are the One who blesses and sanctifies all things, O Christ our God, and to You we give glory, together with Your

Eternal Father and Your All-holy, Good, and Life-giving Spirit, now and forever and to the ages of ages. Amen.

A Prayer After the Midday Meal

We thank You, O Christ our God, for You have filled us this day with Your earthly gifts. Deprive us not of Your heavenly kingdom, but as You came among Your disciples and gave them peace, come among us also, O Savior, and save us. Amen.

Prayer and Blessing
Before the Evening Meal

The poor shall eat and be filled. Those who seek the Lord will praise Him; their hearts shall live forever.

Glory to the Father and to the Son and to the Holy Spirit, both now and forever, and to the ages of ages. Amen.

Lord, have mercy. *(3x)*

O Christ our God, bless the food and drink of Your servants, for You are holy, always, now and forever, and to the ages of ages. AMEN.

ANOTHER BLESSING BEFORE THE EVENING MEAL

LORD JESUS CHRIST OUR GOD, who blessed the five loaves in the wilderness and from them fed five thousand, bless these gifts also, and multiply them in this household and for all Your world, and sanctify Your faithful servants who partake of them. For You are the One who blesses and sanctifies all things, O Christ our God, and to You we give glory, together with Your Eternal Father and Your All-holy, Good, and Life-giving Spirit, now and forever, and to the ages of ages. AMEN.

A PRAYER AFTER THE EVENING MEAL

BLESSED IS GOD, who is merciful to us and feeds us with His bountiful gifts by His divine grace and love for mankind, always, now and forever, and to the ages of ages. AMEN.

LORY TO YOU, O LORD. Glory to You, O Holy One. Glory to You, O King. For You have given us food for joy. Fill us also with Your Holy Spirit, that we may be found well-pleasing before You and not be ashamed when You come to reward each according to his works. AMEN.

(Vespers)

N THE NAME of the Father and of the Son and of the Holy Spirit. AMEN.

THE TRISAGION PRAYERS

OLY GOD, Holy Mighty, Holy Immortal One, have mercy on us. (*3x*)

Glory to the Father and to the Son and to the Holy Spirit, both now and forever and to the ages of ages. AMEN.

O Most Holy Trinity, have mercy on us. O Lord, cleanse us from our sins. O Master, pardon our iniquities. O Holy One, visit and heal our infirmities for Your name's sake.

Lord, have mercy. (*3x*)

Glory to the Father and to the Son and to the Holy Spirit, both now and forever and to the ages of ages. AMEN.

Our Father in heaven, hallowed be Your name. Your kingdom come; Your will be done on earth as it is in heaven. Give us this day our daily bread. And forgive us our trespasses as we forgive those who trespass against us. And lead us not into temptation, but deliver us from the evil one.

Lord, have mercy. *(12x)*

AS I COME to the end of the day, I thank You, O Lord, and I ask that the evening and the night may be free of sin. Grant me this, O Savior, and save me.

Glory to the Father and to the Son and to the Holy Spirit.

As I reach the end of the day, I glorify You, O Master, and I ask that the evening and the night may be free of offense. Grant me this, O Savior, and save me.

Both now and forever, and to the ages of ages. AMEN.

As I pass to the end of the day, I praise You, O Holy
One, and I ask that the evening and the night may be
free of temptation. Grant me this, O Savior, and save me.

Then we may say one or all of the following psalms:

PSALM 103

Bless the Lord, O my soul!
O Lord my God, You have been greatly magnified.
You have clothed Yourself with thanksgiving and majesty.
You have wrapped Yourself in light as with a garment.
You have stretched out the heavens like a curtain.
You are He who covers the upper chambers with waters,
who makes the clouds His mount, who walks on the wings
of the wind,
who makes His angels spirits and His ministers a flame of fire,
who established the earth upon its foundations; throughout
the ages it shall not be moved.
The deep, like a cloak, is its mantle; waters will rest upon the
mountains.
At Your rebuke shall they flee; at the voice of Your thunder
shall they tremble.
The mountains rise and the plains descend to the place which
You established for them.

You fixed a limit that they will not pass, nor will they return to
　　cover the earth.
You send out springs into the valleys; waters shall run between
　　the mountains.
They will give drink to all the beasts of the field;
　　wild donkeys will await them to quench their thirst.
The birds of the air will nest beside them and sing among
　　the rocks.
He waters the mountains from His upper chambers;
　　the earth will be filled from the fruit of His works.
He makes the grass grow for the cattle and green herbs for the
　　service of man;
to bring forth bread from the earth, and wine gladdens the
　　heart of man;
to brighten his face with oil, and bread gives strength to the
　　hearts of men.
The trees of the plain will be satisfied, the cedars of Lebanon,
　　which You planted.
There the sparrows will build their nests; the house of the heron
　　is leader among them.
The high mountains are for the deer; rocks a refuge for hares.
He made the moon to mark the seasons; the sun knows the hour
　　of its setting.
You appointed darkness, and it was night, in which all the
　　beasts of the forest will prowl;
young lions roaring to plunder and to seek their food
　　from God.

*The sun rose and they gathered together, and they will lie down
    in their dens.*

Man shall go out to do his work, to labor until the evening.

Greatly magnified are Your works, O Lord!

*In wisdom You have made them all; the earth was filled with
    Your creation.*

*There is the great, wide sea; there are creeping things without
    number, living creatures both small and great.*

*There ships go to and fro; there is that leviathan which You
    have made to play therein.*

All things look to You to give them their food in due season.

When You give it to them, they will gather it.

*When You open Your hand, all things will be filled with
    goodness.*

But when You turn away Your face, they will be troubled.

*You will take away their spirit, and they will perish and
    return to the dust.*

*You will send forth Your Spirit, and they shall be created,
    and You will renew the face of the earth.*

*Let the glory of the Lord endure forever. The Lord will rejoice
    in His works.*

*He looks upon the earth and makes it tremble. He touches the
    mountains, and they smoke.*

*For as long as I live I will sing to the Lord; for as long as I am
    alive I will praise my God.*

*May my words be pleasing to Him. As for me, I shall rejoice
    in the Lord.*

Oh, that sinners would perish from the earth, and that the
wicked would be no more!
Bless the Lord, O my soul!

Blessed is the man who walks not in the counsel of the ungodly,
nor stands in the path of sinners, nor sits in the place of the
troublesome.
But his will is in the law of the Lord, and on His law he
meditates day and night.
He shall be like a tree that has been planted beside streams of
water, which bears fruit in its season, and its leaves do not
fall; and whatever he does will prosper.
Not so the ungodly, not so: they are like the chaff that the wind
blows from the face of the earth.
Therefore the ungodly will not rise in judgment, nor sinners in
the council of the righteous.
For the Lord knows the way of the righteous, but the way of
the ungodly will perish.

PSALM 140

Lord, I have cried out to You; hear me; hear me, O Lord.
Lord, I have cried out to You; hear me.
Heed the voice of my supplication when I cry.
Let my prayer arise in Your sight as incense.

Let the lifting up of my hands be an evening sacrifice.

Set a guard, O Lord, before my mouth, and a door of enclosure
about my lips.

Incline not my heart to words of evil, to make excuses in sins
with those who work iniquity.

Let me not join with their elect.

The righteous will chastise me with mercy and reprove me;
but let not the oil of sinners anoint my head.

For my prayer is ardent in the presence of their pleasures;
swallowed up by the rocks have their judges been.

They will hear my words, for they are sweet.

As a clod of earth is crushed upon the ground, so have their
bones been scattered before the jaws of hell.

For to You my eyes are turned, O Lord, my Lord; in You have
I hoped; take not away my soul.

Keep me from the snare that they have hidden for me,
and from the traps of evildoers.

Sinners will fall into their own net.

I am alone until I pass them by.

GLORY to the Father and to the Son and to the Holy
Spirit, both now and forever and to the ages of ages.
AMEN.

Then we may say one or all of the following prayers:

An Evening Prayer

Lord, rebuke us not in Your anger, nor chastise us in Your wrath, but deal with us in accordance with Your kindness, O physician and healer of our souls. Lead us to the harbor of Your will. Enlighten the eyes of our heart that we may know Your truth, and grant that the rest of the present day and the whole time of our life may be peaceful and without sin; by the prayers of the holy Mother of God and of all the saints. For Yours is the might and Yours is the kingdom, the power, and the glory, of the Father and of the Son and of the Holy Spirit, now and forever, and to the ages of ages. Amen.

A Prayer of Vespers

Lord, grant that this evening we may be kept without sin. Blessed are You, O Lord, the God of our fathers, and praised and glorified is Your name forevermore. Amen. May Your mercy, O Lord, be upon us, for in You have we put our trust. Blessed are You, O Lord; teach me Your statutes. Blessed are You, O Master; make me understand Your statutes. Blessed

are You, O Holy One; enlighten me with Your statutes.
Lord, Your mercy endures forever: despise not the works
of Your hands. To You is due praise, to You is due song,
to You is due glory, to the Father and to the Son and to
the Holy Spirit, now and forever, and to the ages of ages.
Amen.

A Prayer for Every Hour

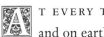T every time and at every hour in heaven
and on earth You are worshipped and glorified,
O Christ our God, You who are longsuffering, most
merciful, most compassionate, who love the just and are
merciful to sinners, who call all to salvation through the
promise of the good things to come. Accept, O Lord, our
entreaties at this hour, and guide our lives that we may
keep Your commandments. Sanctify our souls, purify
our bodies, correct our thoughts, purify our ideas, and
deliver us from all distress, evil, and pain. Surround
us with Your holy angels that, protected and guided by
their host, we may attain unity of faith and the knowledge of Your unapproachable glory. For blessed are You
forever and ever. Amen.

LORD AND MASTER OF MY LIFE, give me not a spirit of sloth, idle curiosity, love of power, and useless chatter. Rather, accord to me, Your servant, a spirit of chastity, humility, patience, and love. Yes, Lord and King, grant that I may see my own faults and not condemn my brother, for blessed are You forever and ever. AMEN.

THROUGH THE PRAYERS of our holy fathers, Lord Jesus Christ our God, have mercy on us and save us. AMEN.

(Compline)

N THE NAME of the Father and of the Son and of the Holy Spirit. AMEN.

O Heavenly King, Comforter, Spirit of Truth, everywhere present and filling all things, Treasury of blessings and Giver of life, come and abide in us, cleanse us from every stain, and save our souls, O Good One.

If it is the Paschal season, the above prayer is replaced by the apolytikion of Pascha:

HRIST IS RISEN from the dead, trampling down death by death, and upon those in the tombs bestowing life.

THE TRISAGION PRAYERS

OLY GOD, Holy Mighty, Holy Immortal One, have mercy on us. *(3x)*

Glory to the Father and to the Son and to the Holy Spirit, both now and forever and to the ages of ages. Amen.

O Most Holy Trinity, have mercy on us. O Lord, cleanse us from our sins. O Master, pardon our iniquities. O Holy One, visit and heal our infirmities for Your name's sake.

Lord, have mercy. *(3x)*

Glory to the Father and to the Son and to the Holy Spirit, both now and forever and to the ages of ages. Amen.

Our Father in heaven, hallowed be Your name. Your kingdom come; Your will be done on earth as it is in heaven. Give us this day our daily bread. And forgive us our trespasses as we forgive those who trespass against us. And lead us not into temptation, but deliver us from the evil one.

Lord, have mercy. *(12x)*

Come, let us worship God our King.
Come, let us worship and fall down before Christ, our King and our God.
Come, let us worship and fall down before Christ Himself, our King and our God.

A Prayer for Forgiveness

Lord our God, if I have sinned in anything this day, in word, or deed, or thought, forgive me all, for You are good, and You love mankind. Grant me peaceful and undisturbed sleep, and deliver me from the assault and attack of the evil one. Rouse me at the proper time to glorify You, for blessed are You, together with Your Only-begotten Son and Your All-holy Spirit, now and forever, and to the ages of ages. Amen.

Evening Intercession

Lord, O Lord, who deliver us from the arrows of temptation that fly by day, deliver us also from every deed of darkness. Accept the lifting up of our hands as an evening sacrifice. Grant that we may also pass through the course of the night without blemish, untried by evil, and deliver us from every trouble and from the fear that comes to us from the devil. Grant penitence to our souls, and let our minds be concerned with Your dread and righteous judgment. Nail down our flesh in fear of You, and mortify our earthly bodies, that in the calm of sleep, we may be made bright by the contemplation of Your judgments. Take from us every unseemly imagination and harmful desire. Raise us up at the time of prayer, strengthened in faith and advancing in Your commandments; through the good pleasure and goodness of Your Only-begotten Son, with whom You are blessed, together with Your All-holy, Good, and Life-giving Spirit, now and forever, and to the ages of ages. AMEN.

Then we may say one or all of the following psalms:

PSALM 50

Have mercy on me, O God, according to Your great mercy, and according to the greatness of Your compassion blot out my offense.
Wash me thoroughly of my iniquity, and cleanse me of my sin.
For I know my iniquity, and my sin is ever before me.
Against You alone have I sinned and done evil in Your sight, that You may be justified in Your words and prevail when You are judged.
For lo, in iniquity I was conceived, and in sins my mother bore me.

*For lo, You have loved truth: the hidden and secret lore of Your
    wisdom have You revealed to me.*

*You will sprinkle me with hyssop, and I shall be cleansed; You
    will wash me, and I shall be made whiter than snow.*

*You will make me hear of joy and gladness; the bones which
    have been humbled will rejoice.*

*Turn away Your face from my sins, and blot out all my
    iniquities.*

*Create a clean heart in me, O God, and renew a right spirit
    within me.*

*Cast me not away from Your presence, and do not take Your
    Holy Spirit from me.*

*Restore to me the joy of Your salvation, and with Your
    sovereign Spirit establish me.*

*I will teach transgressors Your ways, and sinners will turn to
    You again.*

*Deliver me from bloodshed, O God, the God of my salvation,
    and my tongue will rejoice at Your justice.*

*Lord, You will open my lips, and my mouth will proclaim
    Your praise.*

*For if You had desired sacrifice, I would have given it; You will
    not take pleasure in burnt offerings.*

*A sacrifice to God is a broken spirit; a broken and a humbled
    heart God will not despise.*

*Do good to Zion, O Lord, in Your good pleasure; and let the
    walls of Jerusalem be built.*

Then will You be well-pleased with a sacrifice of righteousness,
    with oblations and burnt offerings.
Then will they offer calves upon Your altar.

PSALM 69

O God, come to my aid; O Lord, hasten to help me.
Let those who seek my soul be shamed and confounded.
Let those who wish me evil be turned back and disgraced.
May those who say to me, "Well done, well done!" turn away
    immediately in shame.
Let all who seek You, O God, be glad and rejoice in You.
Let all who love Your salvation ever say, "The Lord be
    magnified."
But I am poor and needy; help me, O God.
You are my helper and my deliverer; O Lord, do not delay.

PSALM 142

O Lord, hear my prayer; heed my supplication in Your truth;
    hear me in Your righteousness.
Enter not into judgment with Your servant, for in Your sight
    shall no man living be justified.
For the enemy has persecuted my soul; he has lowered my life to
    the earth.

He has made me dwell in darkness, like those long dead.

*My spirit grew despondent within me, and my heart within me
  was troubled.*

*I remembered the days of old; I meditated on all Your works:
  I considered the works of Your hands.*

*I stretched out my hands towards You; my soul thirsted for You
  like a waterless land.*

Be quick to hear me, O Lord; my spirit has failed.

*Turn not Your face from me, lest I be like those who go down
  into the pit.*

*Make me hear of Your mercy in the morning, for in You have I
  placed my hope.*

*Make known to me the way I should go, for to You have I lifted
  up my soul.*

*Deliver me from my enemies, O Lord: to You have I fled
  for refuge.*

Teach me to do Your will, for You are my God.

Your good Spirit will guide me in a righteous land.

For the sake of Your name, O Lord, will You quicken me.

*In Your righteousness will You bring my soul out of affliction;
  in Your mercy will You slay my enemies;*

*and You will destroy all those that afflict my soul, for I am
  Your servant.*

Evening Doxology

GLORY TO GOD in the highest, peace on earth, and goodwill among men. We praise You, we bless You, we worship You, we glorify You, we give You thanks for Your great glory: Lord, King, God of heaven, Father Almighty; Only-begotten Son, Lord Jesus Christ; and Holy Spirit. Lord God, Lamb of God, Son of the Father, who take away the sin of the world, have mercy on us, You who take away the sins of the world. Receive our prayer, O You who sit at the right hand of the Father, and have mercy on us. For You alone are holy, You alone are Lord, Jesus Christ, to the glory of God the Father. AMEN.

Every evening will I bless You, and praise Your name forever and to the ages of ages. You have been our refuge, O Lord, from generation to generation. I said, "Lord, have mercy on me; heal my soul, for against You have I sinned." To You have I fled for refuge; teach me to do Your will, for You are my God. For with You is the source of life, and in Your light shall we see light. Let Your mercy remain upon those who know You.

Lord, grant that this night we may be kept without sin. Blessed are You, O Lord, the God of our fathers, and praised and glorified is Your name forevermore. AMEN.

May Your mercy, O Lord, be upon us, for in You have we put our trust. Blessed are You, O Lord; teach me Your statutes. Blessed are You, O Master; make me understand Your statutes. Blessed are You, O Holy One; enlighten me with Your statutes. Lord, Your mercy endures forever: despise not the works of Your hands. To You is due praise, to You is due song, to You is due glory, to the Father and to the Son and to the Holy Spirit, now and forever, and to the ages of ages. AMEN.

THE CREED

I BELIEVE IN ONE GOD, Father Almighty, Maker of heaven and earth and of all things visible and invisible.

And in one Lord Jesus Christ, the Only-begotten Son of God, begotten of the Father before all ages.

Light from Light, true God from true God, begotten not created, of one essence with the Father; through Him all things were made.

For us men and for our salvation He came down from heaven and was incarnate of the Holy Spirit and the Virgin Mary and became man;

He was crucified also for us under Pontius Pilate, and suffered and was buried;

He rose again on the third day, in accordance with the Scriptures, and ascended into heaven, and is seated at the right hand of the Father;

He is coming again in glory to judge the living and the dead; and His kingdom will have no end.

And in the Holy Spirit, the Lord, the Giver of life, who proceeds from the Father, who together with the Father and the Son is worshipped and glorified; who spoke through the Prophets.

In one, Holy, Catholic and Apostolic Church;

I confess one Baptism for the forgiveness of sins;

I expect the resurrection of the dead and the life of the age to come. AMEN.

A Prayer for Every Hour

 T EVERY TIME and at every hour in heaven and on earth You are worshipped and glorified, O Christ our God, You who are longsuffering, most merciful, most compassionate, who love the just and are merciful to sinners, who call all to salvation through the promise of the good things to come. Accept, O Lord, our entreaties at this hour, and guide our lives that we may keep Your commandments. Sanctify our souls, purify our bodies, correct our thoughts, purify our ideas, and deliver us from all distress, evil, and pain. Surround us with Your holy angels that, protected and guided by their host, we may attain unity of faith and the knowledge of Your unapproachable glory. For blessed are You forever and ever. AMEN.

Lord, have mercy. *(3x)*

Glory to the Father and to the Son and to the Holy Spirit, both now and forever, and to the ages of ages. AMEN.

A Prayer to the Mother of God

ECAUSE OF YOU, who are full of grace, all creation rejoices, the ranks of angels and the human race. O hallowed temple, spiritual paradise, and pride of virgins, from you God took flesh, and He who is our God before eternity became a little child, for He made your womb His throne and caused it to become wider than the heavens. Because of you, who are full of grace, all creation rejoices. GLORY TO YOU.

Here we may say the apolytikion of our patron saint or the following prayer:

A Prayer to Our Patron Saint

RAY TO GOD FOR ME, O Holy *(name)*, well-pleasing to God: for I turn to you, who are my swift helper and the intercessor for my soul.

A Prayer to Our Guardian Angel

ANGEL OF CHRIST, holy guardian and protector of my soul and body, forgive me everything wherein I have offended you every day of my life, and protect me from all influence and temptation of the evil one. May I nevermore anger God by any sin. Pray for me to the Lord, that He may make me worthy of the grace of the All-Holy Trinity, of the most-holy Mother of God, and of all the saints.

A Prayer for Forgiveness

REMIT, PARDON, AND FORGIVE, O God, our offenses, both voluntary and involuntary, in deed and in word, in knowledge and in ignorance, by day and by night, in mind and thought; forgive us all things, for You are good, and You love mankind.

Prayer of St. Mardarios

LORD GOD AND MASTER, Father Almighty, Only-begotten Son Jesus Christ, and Holy Spirit, one Godhead, one power, have mercy on me a sinner; and by the judgments which You know, save me, Your unworthy servant. For blessed are You forever and ever. AMEN.

L ORD AND MASTER OF MY LIFE, give me not a spirit of sloth, idle curiosity, love of power, and useless chatter. Rather, accord to me Your servant a spirit of chastity, humility, patience, and love. Yes, Lord and King, grant that I may see my own faults and not condemn my brother, for blessed are You forever and ever. AMEN.

GENERAL INTERCESSION

L ORD, Lover of mankind, forgive those who hate and wrong us. Do good to those who do good. Grant our brethren and kindred their requests that lead to salvation and everlasting life; visit the sick and grant them healing. Guide those at sea. Journey with those who travel. Help Orthodox Christians to struggle. To those who serve and are kind to us grant remissions of sins.

On Your servants *(names of the living),* and on those who have charged us, the unworthy, to pray for them, have mercy according to Your great mercy. Remember, O Lord, Your servants *(names of the departed)*, our fathers and brethren departed before us, and grant them rest where the light of Your countenance shines. Remember, O Lord, our brethren in captivity, and deliver them from every misfortune. Remember, O Lord, those who bring offerings and do good works in Your holy churches, and grant them their requests that lead to salvation and everlasting life. Lord, remember also us, Your lowly, sinful, and unworthy servants, and enlighten our minds with the light of Your knowledge, and guide us in the way of Your commandments; through the intercessions of our most pure Lady the Mother of God and Ever-Virgin Mary, and of all Your saints, for blessed are You forever and ever. AMEN.

If we have received Communion, we may add prayers of thanksgiving after Holy Communion (page 97).

If we are to take Communion in the morning, we may add the canon for Holy Communion (page 67).

PRAYERS BEFORE SLEEP

 LORD who fashioned me, You know well that my invisible enemies do not sleep, and You know the weakness of my miserable flesh, and so into Your hands I commend my spirit. Shelter me with the wings of Your goodness, that I may not sleep unto death. Enlighten the eyes of my mind with the delight of Your divine words, and rouse me at the proper time to give You glory, for You alone are good, and You love mankind.

I shall be sheltered under the shadow of Your wings, and I shall sleep, for You alone, O Lord, have made me dwell in hope.

Into Your hands, O Lord, I entrust my soul and body. Bless me and have mercy on me, and grant me the grace of eternal life.

THROUGH THE PRAYERS of our holy fathers, Lord Jesus Christ our God, have mercy on us and save us. AMEN.

ODE 1

COME, O PEOPLE, let us sing a song to Christ our God, who parted the sea and made a way for the nation He had brought out of captivity in Egypt; for He is glorified.

Have mercy on me, O God, have mercy on me.

May Your holy Body be for me the bread of eternal life, O gracious Lord, and may Your precious Blood be a remedy for every sickness.

Have mercy on me, O God, have mercy on me.

Defiled by misguided deeds, wretch that I am, I am unworthy, O Christ, to partake of Your immaculate Body and divine Blood; but make me worthy of them.

Most holy Mother of God, save us.

O blessed Bride of God, O good land that produced the unplowed Corn that saves the world, grant that I may be saved by eating it.

ODE 3

BY ESTABLISHING ME on the rock of faith, You have given me power over my enemies, and my spirit rejoices when I sing: There is none holy as our God, and none good but You, O Lord.

Have mercy on me, O God, have mercy on me.

Grant me tears to wash the filth from my heart,
O Christ, that, purified and with a good conscience,
I may come with fear and faith to the communion of
Your divine gifts, O Lord.

Have mercy on me, O God, have mercy on me.

Let Your immaculate Body and divine Blood be for the forgiveness of my transgressions, for communion with the Holy Spirit, and for eternal life, O Lover of mankind, and for estrangement from passions and sorrows.

Most holy Mother of God, save us.

O all-holy Lady, altar of the Bread of Life, which for mercy's sake came down from on high and gave new life to the world, make even me, unworthy as I am, worthy now with fear to eat it and live.

ROM A VIRGIN YOU CAME, not as an ambassador nor as an angel, but as the Lord Himself incarnate, and You saved my whole being. Therefore I cry to You: Glory to Your power, O Lord!

Have mercy on me, O God, have mercy on me.

O most merciful One, who were incarnate for us, You willed to be slain as a sheep for the sins of men; therefore, I implore You to blot out my offenses.

Have mercy on me, O God, have mercy on me.

Heal the wounds of my soul, O Lord, and wholly sanctify me, and make me worthy, O Lord, to partake of Your divine mystical Supper, wretched though I am.

Most holy Mother of God, save us.

Intercede for me also, O Lady, to Him who came forth from your womb, and keep me, your servant, pure and blameless, that I may be sanctified by obtaining the spiritual pearl.

ODE 5

 GIVER OF LIGHT and Sovereign Creator of all worlds, guide us in the light of Your commandments, for we know no other god but You.

Have mercy on me, O God, have mercy on me.

As You foretold, O Christ, let it be so for Your unprofitable servant. Abide in me as You promised; for lo, I eat Your divine Body and drink Your Blood.

Have mercy on me, O God, have mercy on me.

O God and Word of God, may the burning coal of Your Body be for my illumination, as I am in darkness, and may Your Blood be for the cleansing of my sinful soul.

Most holy Mother of God, save us.

O Mary, Mother of God, holy tabernacle of the scent of heaven, make me by Your prayers a chosen vessel, that I may partake of the Sacrament of Your Son.

HIRLED ABOUT in the abyss of sin, I appeal to the unfathomable depths of Your compassion: Raise me up from corruption, O God.

Have mercy on me, O God, have mercy on me.

O Savior, sanctify my mind, soul, heart, and body, and grant that I may approach Your fearsome Mysteries without condemnation, O Lord.

Have mercy on me, O God, have mercy on me.

Grant me estrangement from passions, the assistance of Your grace, and assurance of life by the communion of Your Holy Mysteries, O Christ.

Most holy Mother of God, save us.

O God and Holy Word of God, by the prayers of Your holy Mother, sanctify my whole being as I now approach Your divine Mysteries.

Do not disdain me to receive now, O Christ, the Bread that is Your Body and Your divine Blood, and to partake, O Lord, of Your most pure and fearsome Mysteries, wretched though I am. May it not be for my judgment, but for immortality and life everlasting.

HE WISE CHILDREN did not worship the golden idol, but cast themselves into the fire and defied the pagan gods. In the midst of the flames they prayed, and an angel brought them dew, saying: The prayer of your lips has been heard.

Have mercy on me, O God, have mercy on me.

Let the communion of Your immortal Mysteries, the source of all goodness, O Christ, be to me light and life and dispassion, and the means of progress and proficiency in divine virtue, that I may glorify You, O Good One.

Have mercy on me, O God, have mercy on me.

That I may be redeemed from passions, enemies, desires, and all sorrow, I now draw near with trembling, love, and reverence to Your immortal and divine Mysteries, O Lover of mankind. And I sing to You: Blessed are You, O God of our fathers.

Most holy Mother of God, save us.

In a manner beyond understanding you gave birth to Christ the Savior, O you who are full of grace divine. I, your servant, unclean though I am, now beseech you,

O pure one: Cleanse me from all defilement of body and spirit as I approach the immaculate Mysteries.

ODE 8

SING OF THE ACTS OF GOD, who descended into the fiery furnace with the Hebrew children and changed the flame into dew, and exalt Him as Lord throughout the ages.

Have mercy on me, O God, have mercy on me.

In my despair, O Christ, grant that I may partake now of Your heavenly, fearsome, and holy Mysteries and of Your divine Mystical Supper, O God my Savior.

Have mercy on me, O God, have mercy on me.

I seek refuge in Your compassion, O Good One, and I cry to You with fear: Abide in me, O Savior, and I in You, as You said; for lo, confiding in Your mercy, I eat Your Body and drink Your Blood.

Most holy Mother of God, save us.

I tremble as I receive the fire, lest I should burn like wax and hay. O fearsome Mystery! O divine Compassion! How can I who am but clay partake of Your divine Body and Blood and become incorruptible!

ODE 9

HE SON of the Eternal Father, our Lord and God, has appeared to us incarnate of a virgin, to enlighten those in darkness and to gather the scattered. Therefore we magnify the all-hymned Mother of God.

Have mercy on me, O God, have mercy on me.

The Lord is good. O taste and see! For of old He became like us for our sake, and once offered Himself as a sacrifice to His Father, and is perpetually slain, sanctifying those who receive Him.

Have mercy on me, O God, have mercy on me.

May I be sanctified in body and soul, O Lord; may I be enlightened and saved; may I become by the communion of the Holy Mysteries Your dwelling, having You, with the Father and the Spirit, abiding in me, O most merciful Benefactor.

Glory to the Father and to the Son and to the Holy Spirit.

May Your most precious Body and Blood, my Savior, be to me as fire and light, consuming the fuel of sin and burning the thorns of my passions, and enlightening the whole of me to adore Your Divinity.

Both now and forever, and to the ages of ages. AMEN.

God took flesh of your pure blood. Therefore, all generations sing to you, O Lady, and heavenly hosts glorify you. For through you have we clearly seen the Lord of all united with man.

We may say one or all of the following psalms:

PSALM 22

The Lord is my Shepherd, and I shall lack nothing.

He has made me to dwell in green pastures; beside the waters of rest has He nourished me.

He has brought back my soul; He has led me on paths of righteousness for His name's sake.

For though I should walk in the valley of the shadow of death, I will fear no evil, for You are with me; Your rod and Your staff have comforted me.

You have prepared a table before me in the presence of those who afflict me.

You have anointed my head with oil, and Your cup inebriates me.

Your mercy shall follow me all the days of my life, and I will dwell in the house of the Lord forever.

PSALM 23

The earth is the Lord's and the fullness thereof, the world and all that dwells therein.

He has founded it upon the seas, and upon the rivers has He prepared it.

Who shall ascend the mountain of the Lord? Or who shall
stand in His holy place?

He whose hands are innocent and whose heart is pure, who
has not given his soul to vanity, and who has not sworn
deceitfully against his neighbor.

He shall receive a blessing from the Lord and mercy from God
his Savior.

This is the generation of those who seek the Lord, of those who
seek the face of the God of Jacob.

Lift up your gates, O you princes; and be lifted up, you
everlasting gates, and the King of Glory shall enter.

Who is the King of Glory? The Lord, strong and mighty,
the Lord, mighty in war.

Lift up your gates, O you princes; and be lifted up, you
everlasting gates, and the King of Glory shall enter.

Who is the King of Glory? The Lord of hosts, He is the King
of Glory.

PSALM 115

I believed, therefore I spoke; I was humbled exceedingly.
In my amazement I said: Every man is a liar.
What shall I render to the Lord for all that He has given me?
I will take the cup of salvation, and I will call upon the name of
the Lord.
Precious in the sight of the Lord is the death of His holy ones.

*O Lord, I am Your servant; I am Your servant and the son of
Your handmaid.*

You have broken my bonds asunder.

*I will offer a sacrifice of praise to You, and I will call upon the
name of the Lord.*

*I will pay my vows to the Lord in the presence of all His
people; in the courts of the house of the Lord, in the midst
of you, O Jerusalem.*

GLORY TO THE FATHER and to the Son and to the
Holy Spirit, both now and forever, and to the ages of
ages. AMEN.

Alleluia, Alleluia, Alleluia; glory to You, O God. *(3x)*

Lord, have mercy. *(3x)*

Overlook my iniquities, O Lord who were born of a virgin, and purify my heart, and make it a temple for Your
immaculate Body and Blood. Do not cast me away from
Your presence, for great and beyond measure is Your
mercy.

Glory to the Father and to the Son and to the Holy Spirit.

How can I, the unworthy one, have boldness to receive
Your Holy Gifts? For should I dare approach You with
those who are worthy, my garment betrays me, for it is

not fitting for the Supper, and I shall bring condemnation upon my sinful soul. Cleanse the filth of my soul, O Lord, and save me, for You love mankind.

Both now and forever, and to the ages of ages. AMEN.

Great is the multitude of my offenses, O Mother of God; to you have I fled, O pure one, entreating salvation. Visit my ailing soul, and intercede with your Son and our God that He may grant me forgiveness for the grievous deeds which I have committed, O only-blessed one.

Lord, have mercy. *(40x)*

VERSES OF INSTRUCTION

When you, O man, are about to eat the Body of the Master, draw near with fear, lest you be burned: it is fire.
And before you drink the divine Blood to share in communion, reconcile yourself with those who grieve you.
Then, with boldness, venture to eat the Mystic Food.
Before partaking of the dread Sacrifice of the life-giving Body of the Master, pray in this manner with trembling:

Then we may say one or all of the following prayers:

Master, Lord Jesus Christ our God, the Source of life and immortality, who are the Maker of all creation, both visible and invisible, the co-eternal and co-beginningless Son of the Eternal Father, who in the abundance of Your goodness were in the last days clothed in flesh, were crucified and buried for us ungrateful and thankless ones, and by Your own Blood refashioned our nature, which had been corrupted by sin: O Immortal King, accept the repentance even of me, a sinner, and incline Your ear and hear my words.

For I have sinned, O Lord, I have sinned against heaven and before You, and I am not worthy to look upon the height of Your glory; for I have provoked Your goodness by transgressing Your commandments and not obeying Your ordinances. But in Your forbearance, patience, and great mercy, You, O Lord, have not given me up to be destroyed with my sins, but You await my complete conversion.

For You who love mankind have said through Your Prophet that You desire not the death of the sinner, but that he should return to You and live. For You do not will, O Lord, that the work of Your hands should perish, neither do You delight in the destruction of men, but You desire that all should be saved and come to the knowledge of the Truth.

Therefore, though I am unworthy both of heaven and earth, and even of this transient life—since I have completely succumbed to sin and am a slave to pleasure and have defaced Your image—yet being Your work and creation, wretch that I am, even I do not despair of my salvation and dare to draw near to Your boundless compassion.

Therefore, receive even me, O Christ, Lover of mankind, as You received the harlot, the thief, the publican, and the prodigal; and take from me the heavy burden of my sins: You who take away the sin of the world, who heal the infirmities of men, who call the weary and heavy-laden to Yourself and give them rest; for You came not to call the righteous but sinners to repentance. Cleanse me from all defilement of flesh and spirit, and teach me to attain perfect holiness in the fear of You, that with the testimony of a clear conscience I may receive a portion of Your Holy Things and be united with Your holy Body and Blood, and have You dwelling and remaining in me with the Father and Your Holy Spirit.

O Lord Jesus Christ my God, do not let the communion of Your immaculate and life-giving Mysteries be to me for condemnation, nor let it make me sick in body or soul through my partaking of them unworthily; but rather grant that until my last breath I may receive a portion of Your Holy Things without condemnation, for communion with the Holy Spirit, as a provision for eternal life, and as an acceptable defense at Your dread Judgment, so that I, too, with all Your elect may become a partaker of Your pure joys which You have prepared for those who love You, O Lord, in whom You are glorified throughout the ages. AMEN.

SECOND PRAYER

I KNOW, O LORD, that I partake of Your immaculate Body and precious Blood unworthily, that I am guilty, and that I eat and drink judgment to myself by not discerning Your Body and Blood, O Christ my God. Yet, trusting in Your compassion, I take courage and approach You, for You have said, "He who eats My Flesh and drinks My Blood abides in Me and I in him."

Therefore, have compassion, O Lord, and do not make an example of me, a sinner, but deal with me according to Your mercy; and let these Holy Things be for my healing, purification, enlightenment, protection, and salvation; for sanctification of body and soul; for the averting of every delusion, wicked deed, and devilish activity working with intent in my members; for confidence and love toward You; for reformation of life and stability; for an increase of virtue and perfection; for fulfillment of the commandments; for communion with the Holy Spirit; as a provision for eternal life; and as an acceptable defense at Your dread Judgment, not for punishment and condemnation.

THIRD PRAYER

 LORD MY GOD, I know that I am not worthy or sufficient that You should come under the roof of the house of my soul, for all is desolate and fallen, and You do not have within me a place fit to lay Your head. But as You came from on high and humbled Yourself for our sake, so now conform Yourself to my humility.

And as You consented to lie in a cave and in a manger of irrational beasts, so also consent to lie in the manger of my irrational soul and to enter my defiled body.

And as You did not disdain to enter and dine with sinners in the house of Simon the Leper, so consent also to enter the house of my humble soul, which is leprous and sinful.

And as You did not reject the woman who was, like me, a harlot and a sinner, when she approached and touched You, so also be compassionate with me, a sinner, as I approach and touch You.

Let the burning coal of Your most-holy Body and precious Blood be for the sanctification, enlightenment, and strengthening of my humble soul and body; for a relief from the burden of my many sins; for a protection from all diabolical practices; for a restraint and a check on my evil and wicked way of life; for the mortification of the passions; for the keeping of Your commandments; for an increase of Your divine grace; and for the advancement of Your Kingdom. For it is not as one insolent and presumptuous that I draw near to You, O Christ my God, but as one taking courage from Your ineffable goodness, so that having long abstained from communion with You, I may not become a prey to the invisible predator.

Therefore, I pray to You, O Lord, who alone are holy: Sanctify my soul and body, my mind and heart, my emotions and affections, and wholly renew me. Implant in my members the fear of You, and make Your sanctification indelible within me.

Be my helper and defender, guide my life in peace, and make me worthy to stand at Your right hand with Your saints; through the prayers and intercessions of Your all-pure Mother, of Your bodiless ministers and immaculate powers, and of all the saints who have been well-pleasing to You throughout the ages. AMEN.

FOURTH PRAYER

I AM NOT WORTHY, O Lord and Master, that You should enter under the roof of my soul; but since You, in Your love for mankind, do will to dwell in me, I take courage and draw near.

You give the command: I will open the gates which You alone created, that You may enter with love as is Your nature, that You may enter and enlighten my darkened reasoning. I believe that You will do this, for You did not banish the harlot who approached You with tears, nor did You reject the publican who repented, nor did You drive away the thief who acknowledged Your

Kingdom, nor did You abandon the repentant persecutor Paul as he was; but You established all who had been brought to You by repentance in the company of Your friends. For You alone are forever blessed, now and for all eternity. AMEN.

FIFTH PRAYER

LORD JESUS CHRIST my God, loose, remit, forgive, absolve, and pardon the sins, offenses, and transgressions which I, Your sinful, unprofitable, and unworthy servant have committed from my youth up to the present day and hour, whether in knowledge or in ignorance, whether by words or in deeds, whether in my intentions or in my thoughts, and whether by habit or through any of my senses.

And through the prayers of her who conceived You without seed, the all-pure and ever-virgin Mary, Your Mother, my only sure hope and protection and salvation, make me worthy to receive without condemnation Your pure, immortal, life-giving, and fearsome Mysteries, for forgiveness of sins and eternal life; for sanctification and enlightenment; for strength and healing; for health of soul and body; and for the blotting out and disappearance of my evil thoughts, intentions, and prejudices, and the nocturnal visitations of dark and evil spirits.

For Yours is the Kingdom, and to You belong power, glory, honor, and worship, with the Father and the Holy Spirit, now and forever, and to the ages of ages. AMEN.

SIXTH PRAYER

MASTER, LORD JESUS CHRIST our God, who alone have authority to forgive sins, in Your goodness and love for mankind overlook all my offenses, whether committed in knowledge or in ignorance, and make me worthy to receive without condemnation Your divine, glorious, immaculate, and life-giving Mysteries, not for punishment, nor for an increase of sins, but for purification and sanctification, and as a pledge of the life and Kingdom to come, as a protection and help, for the routing of adversaries, and for the blotting out of my many transgressions.

For You are a God of mercy and compassion, and You love mankind, and to You we give glory, with the Father and the Holy Spirit, now and forever, and to the ages of ages. AMEN.

ROM LIPS TAINTED and defiled, from a heart impure and loathsome, from an unclean tongue, and out of a polluted soul, receive my prayer, O my Christ. Do not reject me, nor my words, nor my ways, nor even my shamelessness, but give me courage to say what I desire, O my Christ; and even more, teach me what to do and what to say.

I have sinned more than the harlot who, on learning where You were lodging, bought myrrh and dared to come and anoint Your feet, O Christ, my Lord and my God. As You did not repel her when she drew near in her heart, neither reject me, O Word, but grant that I may clasp and kiss Your feet, and dare to anoint them with a flood of tears as with precious myrrh.

Wash me with my tears and purify me with them, O Word. Forgive my sins and grant me pardon. You know the multitude of my evil deeds. You also know my wounds, and You see my bruises. You also know my faith, and You behold my willingness, and You hear my sighs. Nothing escapes You, my God, my Maker and my Redeemer, not even a teardrop, nor part of a drop.

Your eyes know what I have not achieved, and in Your book things not yet done are written by You.

Look upon my lowliness, and see how great is my trouble. Take from me all my sins, O God of all, that with a clean heart, a trembling mind, and a contrite spirit I may partake of Your pure and all-holy Mysteries, by which all who with sincerity of heart eat and drink are quickened and deified. For You, my Lord, have said, "Whoever eats My Flesh and drinks My Blood abides in Me and I in Him"; wholly true is the word of my Lord and God. For whoever partakes of Your divine and deifying Gifts certainly is not alone, but is with You, my Christ, the Light of the Triune Sun which enlightens the world. That I may not remain alone without You, O Giver of life, my Breath, my Life, my Joy, and the Salvation of the world, I draw near to You, as You see, with tears and with a contrite spirit.

O Ransom of my offenses, I beseech You to receive me, that I may partake without condemnation of Your life-giving and perfect Mysteries, and that You may remain as You have said with me, thrice-wretched though I am, lest the tempter find me without Your grace and craftily seize me and, having deceived me, seduce me from Your deifying words.

Therefore I fall at Your feet and fervently cry to You: as You received the prodigal and the harlot who drew near to You, so also have compassion and receive me, a profligate and a prodigal, as I now approach You with a contrite spirit. I know, O Savior, that no other has sinned against You as I have, nor has any done the deeds that I have committed. But this I also know: that neither the greatness of my offenses nor the multitude of my sins surpasses the great patience of my God and His immense love for man. Despite our offenses, You purify and enlighten with the oil of mercy those who fervently repent, and You make them children of the light and sharers of Your divine nature. You act most generously, for what is strange to angels and to the minds of men You often tell to the repentant as to Your true friends.

These things make me bold, my Christ, these things give me wings, and I take courage from the wealth of Your goodness towards us. With rejoicing, yet with trembling, I who am but straw partake of fire, and oh, strange wonder!—I am ineffably bedewed, like the bush of old which burnt without being consumed. Therefore with a thankful mind and a grateful heart, and with thanksgiving in all the members of my body and soul, I worship and magnify and glorify You, my God, for blessed are You, both now and forevermore.

Eighth Prayer

LORD, YOU ALONE are pure and incorrupt. Through the ineffable compassion of Your love for mankind, You assumed our whole nature through the pure and virgin blood of her who supernaturally conceived You by the coming of the Divine Spirit and by the will of the Eternal Father. O Christ Jesus, Wisdom and Peace and Power of God, You assumed our nature and endured Your life-giving and saving Passion: the Cross, the nails, the spear, and death. Now mortify all the deadly passions of my body.

You who in Your burial despoiled the dominion of hell, bury with good thoughts my evil schemes and scatter the spirits of wickedness.

You who by Your life-giving Resurrection on the third day raised up our fallen Forefather, raise me up who am drowning in sin and set before me ways of repentance.

You who by Your glorious Ascension deified our nature which You had assumed, and honored it by sitting at the right hand of the Father, make me worthy, through partaking of Your holy Mysteries, of a place at Your right hand among those who are saved.

You who by the descent of the Spirit, the Comforter, made Your holy disciples worthy vessels, make me also a recipient of His coming. You who are to come again to judge the world with righteousness, grant that I also may meet You upon the clouds with all Your saints. O my Maker and Creator, let me always glorify and praise You with Your Eternal Father and Your All-holy, Good, and Life-giving Spirit, now and forever, and to the ages of ages. Amen.

Ninth Prayer

I STAND BEFORE the doors of Your sanctuary, yet I do not put away my terrible thoughts. But O Christ our God, who justified the publican, and who had mercy on the Canaanite woman and opened the gates of Paradise to the thief, open to me the depths of Your love for mankind, and as I approach and touch You, receive me as You did the harlot and the woman with an issue of blood. For the one easily received healing by touching the hem of Your garment, and the other obtained release from her sins by clasping Your sacred feet.

And I, deplorable as I am, dare to receive Your whole Body; let me not be burnt, but receive me as You received them. Enlighten the senses of my soul, and burn up the indictments of my sins. By the intercessions of her who bore You without seed, and of the heavenly hosts, for blessed are You forever and ever. AMEN.

IMMEDIATELY BEFORE RECEIVING HOLY COMMUNION

BELIEVE, Lord, and I confess that You are truly the Christ, the Son of the living God, who came into the world to save sinners, of whom I am the first. Moreover, I believe that this is Your immaculate Body and that this is Your precious Blood. Therefore, I pray to You: Have mercy on me and forgive me my transgressions, both voluntary and involuntary, in word and in deed, in knowledge and in ignorance; and make me worthy to partake of Your immaculate Mysteries without condemnation, for the remission of sins and eternal life. Amen.

Behold, I approach for divine Communion;
O Creator, burn me not as I partake;
For You are fire which burns the unworthy.
But rather cleanse me from every impurity.

Of Your Mystical Supper, Son of God, receive me today as a communicant; for I will not speak of the Mystery to Your enemies; I will not give You a kiss, like Judas, but like the thief I confess You: Remember me, Lord, in Your kingdom.

VERSE OF INSTRUCTION

Be stricken with awe, O man, as you look upon the deifying
    Blood;
For it is a burning coal that consumes the unworthy.
The divine Body both deifies and nourishes me;
It deifies the spirit, and wondrously nourishes the mind.

 OU HAVE smitten me with yearning, O Christ, and by Your divine zeal You have changed me; but burn away my sins with immaterial fire, and make me worthy to be filled with delight in You; that, leaping for joy, O Good One, I may magnify Your two comings.

Into the glorious company of Your saints, how shall I the unworthy enter? For if I dare to venture into the bridal chamber, my vesture betrays me, for it is not a wedding garment, and I shall be bound and cast out by the angels. O Lord, cleanse the filth of my soul and save me, for You love mankind.

O Master, Lover of mankind, Lord Jesus Christ my God, do not let these Holy Things be to me for judgment because of my unworthiness, but rather may they be for the purification and sanctification of soul and body, and as a pledge of the life and Kingdom to come. It is good for me to cleave to God, to place in the Lord the hope of my salvation.

Of Your Mystical Supper, Son of God, receive me today as a communicant; for I will not speak of the Mystery to Your enemies; I will not give You a kiss, like Judas, but like the thief I confess You: Remember me, Lord, in Your kingdom.

VERSE OF INSTRUCTION

When you have received the life-giving and mystical Gifts, at once give praise and thanks, and from the bottom of your heart say to God:

Glory to You, O God.
Glory to You, O God.
Glory to You, O God.

Then we may say one or all of the following prayers:

FIRST PRAYER

I THANK YOU, O Lord my God, that You have not rejected me, a sinner, but have made me worthy to partake of Your holy Mysteries.

I thank You that You have permitted me, unworthy though I am, to partake of Your most-pure and heavenly Gifts.

O Master, Lover of mankind, who died and rose for our sake, and granted to us these awesome and life-giving

Mysteries for the well-being and sanctification of our souls and bodies, let these Gifts be for the healing of both soul and body, for the averting of every evil, for the enlightenment of the eyes of my heart, for the peace of the powers of my soul, for faith unashamed, for love unfeigned, for the fullness of wisdom, for the observing of Your commandments, for an increase of Your divine grace, and for the attainment of Your kingdom.

Preserved by them in Your holiness, may I always remember Your grace and no longer live for myself, but for You, our Master and Benefactor.

And thus, when I depart this life in the hope of eternal life, may I attain everlasting rest, where the feast of those who rejoice is unceasing, and the delight of those who behold the ineffable beauty of Your countenance is unending.

For You are the true joy and inexpressible gladness of those who love You, O Christ our God, and all creation praises You forever. AMEN.

Second Prayer

Master, Christ our God, King of the ages and Creator of all things, I thank You for all the good gifts You have given me, and especially for the communion of Your pure and life-giving Mysteries.

Therefore I pray to You, O Good Lord and Lover of mankind: Keep me under the protection and in the shadow of Your wings; grant that even to my last breath I may with a pure conscience partake worthily of Your Holy Gifts for the remission of sins and for eternal life.

For You are the Bread of life, the Source of holiness, the Giver of all good things, and to You we give glory, together with the Father and the Holy Spirit, now and forever, and to the ages of ages. Amen.

Third Prayer

You have willingly given me Your Flesh for food, You who are a burning fire to the unworthy. Consume me not, O my Creator.

Rather enter my very being, my limbs, my joints, my organs, and my heart.

Burn all my iniquities like thorns; cleanse my soul, make holy my thoughts, make firm my knees and my bones as well.

Enlighten my five senses and make vigilant my entire being with the fear of You.

Watch over me always; shield and protect me from every deed and word which corrupts the soul.

Cleanse me, purify me, and put me in order; adorn me, give me understanding, and enlighten me.

Show me to be the dwelling of Your Spirit alone, and not the dwelling place of sin; so that, as I am the vessel of Holy Communion, every evildoer and every passion will flee from me as from fire.

As intercessors I bring to You all the saints, the leaders of the bodiless hosts, Your Forerunner, the wise apostles, and with them Your most pure and holy Mother; accept their prayers, my compassionate Christ, and make Your servant a child of light.

For in Your goodness, O God and Master, You sanctify and enlighten our souls, and it is proper to send up glory to You each day.

O LORD JESUS CHRIST OUR GOD, let Your sacred Body bring me eternal life, and Your precious Blood remission of sins. Let this Eucharist be to me for joy, health, and gladness. And at Your dread Second Coming make me, a sinner, worthy to stand at the right hand of Your glory, through the intercessions of Your all-pure Mother and of all the saints. AMEN.

A PRAYER TO THE MOTHER OF GOD

ALL-HOLY LADY, MOTHER OF GOD, light of my darkened soul, my hope, shelter, refuge, comfort, and joy: I thank you, for you have deemed me, the unworthy one, worthy to partake of the most-pure Body and precious Blood of your Son.

You who gave birth to the true Light, enlighten the spiritual eyes of my heart; you who conceived the Source of immortality, revive me who am dead in sin; you who are the compassionate Mother of the merciful God, have mercy on me and grant me penitence and contrition of heart, humility in my ideas, and release from the imprisonment of my thoughts.

And grant me, until my last breath, to receive without condemnation the sanctification of the most-pure Mysteries for the healing of both soul and body.

Grant me tears of repentance and confession that I may praise and glorify you all the days of my life.

For you are blessed and glorified forever. AMEN. *(3x)*

THE PRAYER OF THE RIGHTEOUS SIMEON

NOW YOU LET YOUR SERVANT depart in peace, O Master, according to Your word. For my eyes have seen Your salvation, which You have prepared before the face of all peoples: a light of revelation to the nations, and the glory of Your people, Israel.

THE TRISAGION PRAYERS

OLY GOD, Holy Mighty, Holy Immortal One, have mercy on us. *(3x)*

Glory to the Father and to the Son and to the Holy Spirit, both now and forever and to the ages of ages. AMEN.

O Most Holy Trinity, have mercy on us. O Lord, cleanse us from our sins. O Master, pardon our iniquities. O Holy One, visit and heal our infirmities for Your name's sake.

Lord, have mercy. *(3x)*

Glory to the Father and to the Son and to the Holy Spirit, both now and forever and to the ages of ages. AMEN.

Our Father in heaven, hallowed be Your name. Your kingdom come; Your will be done on earth as it is in heaven. Give us this day our daily bread. And forgive us our trespasses as we forgive those who trespass against us. And lead us not into temptation, but deliver us from the evil one.

Then we may say one of the following prayers
(to the saint to whom the Liturgy is attributed):

For the Liturgy of St. John Chrysostom

RACE HAS SHONE FORTH from your mouth like fire, illuminating the inhabited world. You stored up for the world the treasure of freedom from avarice and revealed to us the heights of humility. Having taught us by your words, O Father John Chrysostom, implore Christ the Word and our God to save our souls.

You received divine grace from heaven, and with your words you teach us all to worship one God in Trinity, O all-blessed and venerable John Chrysostom. Rightly do we praise you, for you are a teacher who makes clear things divine.

For the Liturgy of St. Basil the Great

YOUR VOICE HAS ECHOED throughout the world, for it has received the words through which you instructed us in a manner worthy of God. You made clear the nature of things and established a rule of life for men. O venerable father and kingly priest, implore Christ our God to save our souls.

You stood as an unshakable pillar of the Church, upholding its authority as a sure refuge for mortal men and sealing it with your doctrines, O venerable Basil, revealer of heaven.

For the Liturgy of the Presanctified Gifts (St. Gregory the Great)

OU RECEIVED GRACE from God above, O glorious Gregory, and you were strengthened with its power. You willed to walk in the path of the Gospel, O most blessed one. Therefore you have received from Christ the reward of your labors. Entreat Him that He may save our souls.

You showed yourself to be an imitator of Christ, the Chief Shepherd, O Father Gregory, guiding monks to the fold of heaven. You taught the flock of Christ His commandments. Now you rejoice and feast with them in the mansions on high.

For the Liturgy of St. James

As a disciple of the Lord you received the Gospel, O righteous James; as a martyr you had unfailing courage; as the brother of God, you have boldness; as a hierarch, you have the power to intercede. Therefore pray to Christ our God that our souls may be saved.

When God the Word, the Only-begotten of the Father, came to live among us in these last days, He declared you, O venerable James, to be the first shepherd and teacher of Jerusalem, and a faithful steward of the spiritual Mysteries. Therefore we all honor you, O holy Apostle.

Through the intercession of the Mother of God and of all Your saints, grant us Your peace, O Lord, and have mercy on us, for You alone are compassionate.

Lord, have mercy. (12x)

Glory to the Father and to the Son and to the Holy Spirit, both now and forever, and to the ages of ages. Amen.

To the Mother of God

GREATER IN HONOR than the cherubim, and beyond compare more glorious than the seraphim, undefiled you gave birth to God the Word: truly the Mother of God, we magnify you.

Through the prayers of our holy fathers, Lord Jesus Christ our God, have mercy on us and save us. AMEN.

ITH THE SPIRITS of the righteous made perfect, give rest, O Savior, to the souls of Your servants, keeping them in a blessed life with You, O Lover of mankind.

In blessed repose where all Your saints find peace, give rest, O Lord, to the souls of Your servants, for You alone are immortal.

Glory to the Father and to the Son and to the Holy Spirit.

You are our God, who descended into hell and released the bonds of those held fast in anguish. Give rest, O Savior, to the souls of Your servants.

Both now and forever, and to the ages of ages. AMEN.

O only pure and spotless Virgin, who bore God without seed, intercede for the salvation of the souls of your servants.

With the saints give rest, O Christ, to the souls of Your servants, where there is neither pain, nor sorrow, nor sighing, but life everlasting.

REMEMBER, O LORD, our fathers and brethren who have fallen asleep in the hope of resurrection unto everlasting life, and all who have died in piety and faith, and pardon them every sin they have committed, willingly or unwillingly, in word or deed or thought. Settle them in a place of light, a place of refreshment, a place of repose, whence pain, grief, and sighing have fled away, and where the light of Your countenance gives gladness to all Your saints throughout the ages. Grant them and us Your kingdom, participation in Your ineffable blessings, and the enjoyment of Your endless and blessed life. For You are the life, the resurrection, and the repose of Your sleeping servants, O Christ our God, and to You we give glory, together with Your Eternal Father, and Your All-holy, Good, and Life-giving Spirit, now and forever, and to the ages of ages. AMEN.

Remember, O Lord, for You are good, Your servants *(names),* and forgive them all the sins they have committed in life; for You alone are without sin, and You alone are able to give rest to the departed.

A Prayer for
Non-Orthodox Departed

LORD, the only Creator, who in the depth of Your wisdom provide all things out of love for mankind, and grant unto all what is profitable: give rest to the souls of *(names),* for You, O God, made them and fashioned them.

A Prayer for the Bereaved

ORD, O LORD, consolation of the afflicted, comfort of those who mourn, and help of all in distress: in Your compassion console those who are afflicted by grief for the departed; heal all the pain of sorrow that lies heavy on their hearts, and to *(name)* who has fallen asleep give rest. For You are the repose of the departed, and to You we give glory, to the Father and to the Son and to the Holy Spirit, now and forever, and to the ages of ages. AMEN.

Before Confession

PSALM 50

*Have mercy on me, O God, according to Your great mercy,
and according to the greatness of Your compassion blot out
my offense.*

Wash me thoroughly of my iniquity, and cleanse me of my sin.

For I know my iniquity, and my sin is ever before me.

*Against You alone have I sinned and done evil in Your sight,
that You may be justified in Your words and prevail when
You are judged.*

*For lo, in iniquity I was conceived, and in sins my mother
bore me.*

*For lo, You have loved truth: the hidden and secret lore of Your
wisdom have You revealed to me.*

*You will sprinkle me with hyssop, and I shall be cleansed; You
will wash me, and I shall be made whiter than snow.*

*You will make me hear of joy and gladness; the bones which
have been humbled will rejoice.*

*Turn away Your face from my sins, and blot out all my
iniquities.*

Create a clean heart in me, O God, and renew a right spirit
within me.

Cast me not away from Your presence, and do not take Your
Holy Spirit from me.

Restore to me the joy of Your salvation, and with Your
sovereign Spirit establish me.

I will teach transgressors Your ways, and sinners will turn to
You again.

Deliver me from bloodshed, O God, the God of my salvation,
and my tongue will rejoice at Your justice.

Lord, You will open my lips, and my mouth will proclaim
Your praise.

For if You had desired sacrifice, I would have given it; You will
not take pleasure in burnt offerings.

A sacrifice to God is a broken spirit; a broken and a humbled
heart God will not despise.

Do good to Zion, O Lord, in Your good pleasure;
and let the walls of Jerusalem be built.

Then will You be well-pleased with a sacrifice of righteousness,
with oblations and burnt offerings.

Then will they offer calves upon Your altar.

THE PRAYER OF MANASSEH

LORD ALMIGHTY, the God of our Fathers, of
Abraham, Isaac, and Jacob, and of their righteous

seed; who made heaven and earth with all their array; who fastened the sea by the word of Your command; who shut up the deep and sealed it with Your fearsome and glorious name; before whom all things shudder and tremble in the presence of Your power; for unbearable is the magnificence of Your glory, and not to be withstood is the anger of Your threat toward sinners, and the mercy of Your promise is measureless and unsearchable. For You are the Lord Most High, compassionate, long-suffering, and abounding in mercy, and You repent toward the evil deeds of men. O Lord, according to the greatness of Your goodness have You appointed repentance and forgiveness to those who have sinned against You, and in the greatness of Your compassion have You decreed repentance unto salvation for sinners. Therefore, O Lord God of Powers, You did not appoint repentance for the righteous, for Abraham, Isaac, and Jacob, who did not sin against You, but You have appointed repentance for me, a sinner. For I have sinned more than the measure of sand in the sea. My iniquities have been multiplied, O Lord, my iniquities have been multiplied, and I am not worthy to raise my eyes and to behold the height of heaven, because of the multitude of my unrighteous deeds. I am bowed down by a heavy iron fetter, so that I cannot lift my head, and there is no relief for me; for I have provoked Your wrath and done what is evil in Your sight; I have not done Your will nor kept Your commandments. And now I bend the knee of my heart, begging for Your clemency. I have sinned, O Lord, I have sinned, and I know my iniquities. I am asking, begging You: Forgive me, O Lord, forgive me! Destroy me not in my transgressions; be not angry with me forever, nor condemn me to the depths of the earth, for You, O Lord, are the God of those who repent. And in me You will show all Your goodness, for, though I am unworthy, You will save me according to Your great mercy. And I will praise You all the days of my life. For all the powers of heaven sing Your praises, and glory is Yours forevermore.

A Prayer of Repentance

Lord my God, I confess that I have sinned against You in thought, in word, and in deed. I have also omitted to do what Your holy law requires of me. But now in repentance and contrition I turn again to Your love and mercy. I entreat You: Forgive me all my transgressions and cleanse me from all my sins. Fill my heart with the light of Your truth, O Lord. Strengthen my will by Your grace, and teach me both to desire and to do only what is pleasing to You. Amen.

A Thanksgiving Prayer after Confession

Lord, my Savior and Master, I, Your unprofitable servant, with fear and trembling give thanks to You for Your lovingkindness and for all the benefits You have poured so abundantly upon me. I fall down in adoration before You, O God, and I offer You my praise. Enlighten my mind and guard all my senses, that henceforth I may walk in righteousness and keep Your commandments, that I may finally attain eternal life with You, the source of life, and be admitted to the glory of Your unapproachable Light; for You are my God, and to You I give glory, to the Father and to the Son and to the Holy Spirit, now and forever, and to the ages of ages. Amen.

SPIRITUAL LIFE

BEFORE READING THE SCRIPTURES OR OTHER SPIRITUAL TEXTS

LORD JESUS CHRIST, open the eyes of my heart, that I may hear Your word and that I may understand and do Your will, for I am a sojourner upon the earth. Hide not Your commandments from me, but open my eyes, that I may perceive the wonders of Your law. Reveal to me the hidden and secret lore of Your wisdom. In You, O God, do I place my hope. Enlighten my mind and understanding with the light of Your knowledge, not only to cherish those things that are written, but to do them; that in reading the lives and sayings of the saints I may not sin, but that such may serve for my renewal, enlightenment, and sanctification, for the salvation of my soul and the inheritance of everlasting life. For You are the enlightenment of those who lie in darkness, and from You comes every good deed and every gift. AMEN.

Before Reading the Gospel

Master, Lover of mankind, make the pure light of Your divine knowledge shine in our hearts, and open the eyes of our mind that we may understand the message of Your Gospel. Implant in us the fear of Your blessed commandments, so that, having trampled down all carnal desires, we may pursue a spiritual way of life, thinking and doing all things that are pleasing to You. For You are the illumination of our souls and bodies, O Christ our God, and to You we give glory, together with Your Eternal Father and Your All-holy, Good, and Life-giving Spirit, now and forever, and to the ages of ages. Amen.

On Entering a Church (Psalm 83)

How beloved are Your dwellings, O Lord of hosts;
my soul longs and faints for the courts of the Lord.
My heart and my flesh rejoiced in the living God.
For the sparrow has found himself a home, and the dove a nest
for herself, where she may lay her young:
Your altars, O Lord of hosts, my King and my God.
Blessed are those who dwell in Your house; they will praise You
forever.

*Blessed is he whose help is from You; who has set steps in his
heart, to rise from the valley of weeping to the place that
has been prepared.*

*For the lawgiver will give blessings; they will go from strength
to strength; the God of gods will appear in Zion.*

*O Lord God of powers, hear my prayer; give heed, O God
of Jacob.*

*Behold our shield, O God; and look upon the face of
Your Christ.*

*For one day in Your courts is better than a thousand
outside them.*

*I chose to be cast aside in the house of my God, rather than to
dwell in the tents of sinners.*

O Lord God of hosts, blessed is he who hopes in You.

On Leaving a Church
(The Prayer of the Righteous Simeon)

NOW YOU LET YOUR SERVANT DEPART in
peace, O Master, according to Your word. For my
eyes have seen Your salvation, which You have prepared
before the face of all peoples: a light of revelation to the
nations, and the glory of Your people, Israel.

The Jesus Prayer

Lord Jesus Christ, Son of God, have mercy on me, a sinner.

or

Lord Jesus Christ, Son of God, have mercy on us.

Work, Study, and Recreation

Before a Journey

 Lord Jesus Christ my God, be my companion, guide, and protector on my journey. Keep me from all danger, misfortune, and temptation. By Your divine power, grant me a peaceful voyage and safe arrival. For in You I place my hope, and to You I give glory, to the Father and to the Son and to the Holy Spirit, now and forever, and to the ages of ages. Amen.

Before Work

Lord Jesus Christ, Only-begotten Son of the Eternal Father, You have said, "Without Me you can do nothing." In faith I embrace Your words, O Lord, and bow before Your goodness. Grant me the inclination to be fruitful in labor, and bless my work for Your glory. Amen.

After Work

Thank You, O Lord, for Your strength and guidance in my work. You are the fulfillment of all good things. Fill also my soul with joy and gladness, that I may praise You, Father, Son, and Holy Spirit, always, now and forever, and to the ages of ages. Amen.

Before Study

Christ my Lord, Giver of light and wisdom, who opened the eyes of the blind man and made the fishermen wise heralds and teachers of the Gospel through the coming of the Holy Spirit, illuminate also my mind with the light of the grace of Your Holy Spirit.

Grant me discernment, understanding, and wisdom in learning, that I may abound in every good work and glorify You, together with Your Eternal Father, and Your All-holy, Good, and Life-giving Spirit, always, now and forever, and to the ages of ages. AMEN.

BEFORE USING THE INTERNET

BE THE HELPER OF MY SOUL, O God, for I walk in the midst of many snares. Deliver me from them and save me, for You are good, and You love mankind.

SICKNESS AND HEALTH

PRAYER OF A SICK PERSON

JESUS CHRIST, my Lord and Savior, You became man and died on the cross for our salvation. You healed people of sickness and affliction through Your love and compassion. Visit me, O Lord, and grant me strength to bear this sickness with which I am afflicted with patience, submission to Your will, and trust in Your loving care. Bless the means used for my recovery and those who administer them. Let my sickness be for the benefit of my soul, and grant that I may live the rest of my life according to Your will. For You are the source of life and healing, and to You I give praise and glory, now and forevermore. Amen.

Prayer for a Sick Person

Heavenly Father, physician of our souls and bodies, who have sent Your Only-begotten Son and our Lord Jesus Christ to heal every sickness and infirmity, visit and heal also Your servant *(name)* from all sickness of soul and body through the grace of Your Christ. Grant him/her patience in sickness, strength of body and spirit, and recovery of health. For You, O Lord, have taught us through Your word to pray for each other that we may be healed. Therefore I pray, heal Your servant *(name)* and grant him/her the gift of complete health. For You are the source of healing, and to You I give glory, Father, Son, and Holy Spirit. Amen.

Thanksgiving after Recovery

LMIGHTY GOD and Heavenly Father, You are the fountain of life and healing. I bless Your holy name and offer You thanks for delivering me from sickness and restoring me to health. Grant me Your eternal grace, I pray, that I may live a new life in true obedience to You. Guide me to do Your will in all things, devoting my life to Your service. Thus living for You, let me be found worthy of Your kingdom, where You dwell in glory with Your Son and Your Holy Spirit forever. AMEN.

Before an Operation

HEAVENLY FATHER, Creator and Comforter, who created me in Your image and likeness, You know every fiber of my being and have willed me into existence. I implore You, O Lord, to guide the minds and hands of those who will operate on me so that I may be restored to health and well-being. Help me, O Lord, to pray with all my heart, and relieve the burden of concern and anxiety that rests heavily upon me and my family with the knowledge that You are with us, now and always. And when I awake from surgery, take me by Your hand, O Lord, and lead me to a life of peace and thanksgiving. AMEN.

AFTER AN OPERATION

COMPASSIONATE LORD, I thank You because You have aided and guided all who assisted in my healing and recovery. Like the woman who touched the hem of Your garment, I too have been freed from the anxiety and isolation of my illness. Bless me, O Lord, with the lovingkindness You so abundantly pour upon me, that I may continuously bear witness to Your healing grace. For blessed and glorified are You forever and ever. AMEN.

FOR THE TERMINALLY ILL

LORD, JESUS CHRIST, who suffered and died for our sins that we may live, in Your love and goodness forgive Your servant *(name)* every sin he/she has committed in life, in word, deed, or thought. All our hope we place in You. Therefore look upon Your servant *(name)* and keep him/her from all evil. We submit to

Your will, and into Your hands we commend our souls and bodies. For a Christian end to our lives, painless, unashamed, and peaceful, and for a good defense before Your fearsome judgment seat, we pray to You, O Lord. Therefore bless us, be merciful to us, and grant us everlasting life. AMEN.

MARRIAGE AND FAMILY

PRAYER OF A SINGLE PERSON SEEKING A SPOUSE

ALL-GOOD AND MERCIFUL LORD, I know that any enduring happiness in my life depends upon my wholehearted love for You and upon my actions according to Your holy will in all things; therefore, guide my soul, O God, and fill my heart. I seek to please You alone, for You are my Creator and my God. Preserve me from pride and self-love. Let reason, modesty, and chastity adorn me.

Your law commands that man and wife live in chaste matrimonial union; therefore, lead me, O Holy Father, to this blessed calling, not for the satisfaction of passions but for the fulfillment of Your commandment; for You have said that it is not good that man should live alone upon the earth, and, having created woman as his helper, You blessed them to be fruitful and multiply that they may fill the earth.

Hear my humble prayer from the depths of my heart: Bestow upon me an honest and devout spouse, so that together, through our love and harmony, we may praise You, our compassionate God, the Father, Son, and Holy Spirit, now and forevermore. Amen.

Prayer of a Married Couple

MERCIFUL GOD, we beseech You ever to remind us that the married state is holy, and that we must keep it so. Grant us Your grace, that we may continue in faithfulness and love; increase in us the spirit of mutual understanding and trust, that no quarrel or strife may come between us; grant us Your blessings, that we may stand before others and in Your sight as an ideal family; and in Your mercy, account us worthy of everlasting life. For You are our sanctification, and to You we give glory, to the Father and to the Son and to

the Holy Spirit, now and forever, and to the ages of ages.
AMEN.

ON MOVING INTO A NEW HOME

GOD OUR SAVIOR, You deigned to enter under the roof of Zacchaeus for his salvation and for the salvation of all in his house. Now, O Lord, keep us who have desired to dwell here safe from all harm, and accept our supplication, unworthy though we are. Bless this habitation, and keep our lives free from all evil. For to You are due all glory, honor, and worship, together with Your Eternal Father, and Your All-holy, Good, and Life-giving Spirit, now and forever, and to the ages of ages. AMEN.

PRAYER OF A MARRIED COUPLE TRYING TO CONCEIVE

GOD MOST PURE, Maker of all creation, in Your love for mankind You transformed the rib of our forefather Adam into a woman, and blessed them and said, "Be fruitful and multiply, and have dominion over the earth." You blessed Your servant Abraham by granting Sarah offspring and made him the father of

many nations; You gave Isaac to Rebecca and blessed
their child; You joined Jacob to Rachel and from them
brought forth the twelve Patriarchs; You united Joseph
and Asenath and granted them Ephrem and Manasseh as
offspring; You heard Zachariah and Elizabeth and made
their child the Forerunner; and from the root of Jesse
You brought forth the Ever-virgin Mary, from whom
You became incarnate and were born for the salvation of
the human race.

Therefore we implore You, O Master, grant us fruit of
the womb, the gift of abundant fertility, and the blessing
of well-favored children, for blessed are You, together
with Your Eternal Father and Your All-holy, Good, and
Life-giving Spirit, now and forever, and to the ages of
ages. AMEN.

PRAYER OF A PREGNANT WOMAN

I THANK YOU, O Sovereign Lord, Jesus Christ
our God, the Source of life and immortality, for
in my marriage You have bestowed upon me Your blessing and gift; for You, O Master, said, "Be fruitful and
multiply and have dominion over the earth." I implore
You, O Lover of mankind: Bless me and the fruit of my

womb, and bring me to a safe delivery. May I give birth to a fruitful vine to be a cause of joy to me all the days of my life. For blessed are You, together with Your Only-begotten Son and Your All-holy, Good, and Life-giving Spirit, now and forever, and to the ages of ages. AMEN.

FOR A WOMAN UNDERGOING A DIFFICULT LABOR

LORD GOD ALMIGHTY, Creator of all things and Giver of knowledge to mankind: You fashioned the body of man from the earth and breathed into his nostrils the breath of life, granting him Your blessings, that he might increase and multiply by means of the birth of children. We fervently entreat You who love mankind to bless this Your servant, *(name),* who is with child, granting her help and comfort at this trying time. Ease her labor and bring her to a safe delivery. Yes, O Lord, open to her the treasury of Your mercy and compassion, and let her give birth to a fruitful vine to be a cause of joy to her all the days of her life. For blessed are You, together with Your Only-begotten Son and Your All-holy, Good, and Life-living Spirit, now and forever, and to ages of ages. AMEN.

Prayer of a Husband and Wife after Giving Birth to a Child

Lord our God, who freely chose to descend from heaven and to be born of the holy Mother of God and Ever-virgin Mary for the salvation of us sinners: You are the One who said, "Increase and multiply, and have dominion over the earth." Therefore bless us and this, our child, O Lord, and grant that Your holy name may remain indelible upon him/her. At the proper time, let him/her be attached to Your Church and be perfected by the awesome Mysteries of Your Christ, that he/she may attain the blessedness of the elect in Your kingdom. For You are the One who guards infants, O Lord, and to You we give glory, to the Father and to the Son and to the Holy Spirit, now and forever, and to the ages of ages. Amen.

A Prayer of Parents for Their Children

God, our heavenly Father, who love mankind and are most merciful and compassionate, have mercy on Your servants, *(names),* for whom we humbly pray and whom we commend to Your gracious care and protection. Be their guide and guardian in all their endeavors, O God, lead them in the way of Your truth, and draw them nearer to You, that they may lead a godly and righteous life in love and fear of You, doing Your will in all things. Give them grace to be temperate, industrious, diligent, devout, and charitable. Defend them against the wiles of the enemy, grant them wisdom and strength to resist all temptation and corruption, and lead them in the way of salvation. Through the compassion of Your Only-begotten Son, with whom You are blessed, together with Your All-holy, Good, and Life-giving Spirit, now and forever, and to the ages of ages. AMEN.

FOR A WOMAN AFTER A MISCARRIAGE

SOVEREIGN MASTER, Lord our God, who were born of the all-pure Mother of God and Ever-virgin Mary, and as an infant were laid in a manger: do You Yourself, according to Your great mercy, have regard for this Your servant *(name)* who has miscarried that which was conceived in her. Heal her suffering, granting to her, O loving Lord, health and strength of body and soul. Guard her with a shining angel from every assault of sickness and weakness and all inward torment. O You who accept the innocence of infancy in Your kingdom, comfort the mind of Your servant and bring her peace. AMEN.

FOR A DEPARTED CHILD AFTER A MISCARRIAGE

REMEMBER, O Lord and Lover of mankind, the soul of Your departed child, which has died in the womb of its mother. Baptize him/her, O Lord, in the sea of Your generosity and save him/her by Your ineffable grace. AMEN.

FOR A BABY WHO HAS DIED BEFORE BAPTISM

REMEMBER, O LORD and Lover of mankind, the soul of Your child, (*name*), departed from us before he/she could receive the Holy Sacrament of Baptism. Baptize him/her, O Lord, in the sea of Your generosity, and save him/her by Your ineffable grace. AMEN.

Trials and Temptations

For the Protection of Soldiers During War

 Holy Master, almighty Father and pre-eternal God, You alone made and commanded all things; You rise up quickly against the evil of the impious, and by Your providence You teach Your people to uphold justice and to turn swords into ploughshares; You commanded the Forerunner John to say to the soldiers coming to him in the desert, "Do not intimidate anyone" and "Be content with your wages." In contrition we entreat You who gave Your child David the power to defeat Goliath, and who condescended, through Judas the Maccabee, to seize victory from the arrogant heathens who would not call on Your name: protect in righteousness and truth Your servants against the enemies rising against them, and by Your lovingkindness, grant them strength and might to uphold faith and truth.

In Your mercy, O Master, teach them the fear of You, and grant them humility, obedience, and endurance. Let them kill no one unjustly, but rather let them preserve all righteousness and truth. May they run in friendship to those who are scattered, extending Your love to those near them, upholding the weak with righteousness, and may their ranks fulfill all things justly.

For You are our God, and to You do we give glory, to the Father and to the Son and to the Holy Spirit, now and forever, and to the ages of ages. Amen.

For Times of Need

LMIGHTY GOD, Father of mercy and God of all consolation, come to my aid and deliver me from all adversity. For I believe, O Lord, that all trials of this life are under Your care, and that all things work for the good of those who love You. Take away from me fear, anxiety, and distress. Help me to face and endure my difficulties with faith, courage, and wisdom. Grant that this trial may bring me closer to You, for You are my rock and my refuge, my comfort and my hope, my delight and my joy. In Your love and compassion do I place my trust. For blessed is Your name, of the Father, and of the Son, and of the Holy Spirit, now and forevermore. Amen.

For Times of Trouble

L ORD OF HOSTS, be with us. For in times of distress we have no other help but You. O Lord of hosts, have mercy on us.

Thanksgiving after Deliverance from Trouble

A LMIGHTY AND MERCIFUL GOD, I most humbly and heartily thank Your divine majesty for Your lovingkindness and tender mercy, for You have heard my humble prayer and graciously granted me deliverance from my trouble and misery. I entreat You to continue granting Your helping grace, that I may lead a life pleasing to You, and that I may continually offer to You a sacrifice of praise and thanksgiving, to the Father and to the Son and to the Holy Spirit, now and forevermore. AMEN.

For Times of Temptation

J ESUS CHRIST, Sovereign Master, help me and do not let me sin against You. Incline not my heart to words or thoughts of evil, but deliver me from all temptation. AMEN.

Prayer of St. Aidan of Lindisfarne

EAVE ME ALONE WITH GOD as much as
may be.

As the tide draws the waters close in upon the shore,

Make me an island, set apart,

   Alone with You, O God, holy to You.

Then with the turning of the tide

Prepare me to carry Your presence to the busy world
   beyond,

The world that rushes in on me,

   Till the waters come again and take me back to You.

Prayers of St. Ambrose of Milan

A Healing Prayer

Y OU ALONE I FOLLOW, Lord Jesus; You heal my wounds. For what shall separate me from the love of God, which is in You? Shall tribulation, or distress, or famine? I am held fast as though by nails and fettered by the bonds of charity. Remove from me, O Lord Jesus, with Your powerful sword, the corruption of my sins. Secure me in the bonds of Your love; cut away what is corrupt in me. Come quickly and make an end of my many hidden and secret afflictions. Open the wound lest the evil sickness spread. With Your purity, cleanse in me all that is stained. Hear me, O you earthly men, who in your sins bring forth drunken thoughts: I have found a Physician. He dwells in heaven and distributes His healing on earth. He alone can heal my pains who Himself has none. He alone who knows what is hidden can take away the grief of my heart and the fear of my soul: Jesus Christ. Christ is grace! Christ is life! Christ is resurrection! AMEN.

A Prayer before Holy Communion

 Lord Jesus Christ, I approach Your banquet table in fear and trembling, for I am a sinner, and dare not rely on my own worth but only on Your goodness and mercy. I am defiled by many sins in body and soul, and by my unguarded thoughts and words. O Gracious God of majesty and awe, I seek Your protection, I look for Your healing. Poor and troubled sinner that I am, I appeal to You, the fountain of all mercy. I cannot bear Your judgment, but I trust in Your salvation. I show my wounds to You, O Lord, and I reveal my shame before You. I know my sins are great and many, and they fill me with fear; yet I hope in Your mercy, for it cannot be measured. O Lord Jesus Christ, Eternal King, God and Man, who were crucified for mankind, look upon me with mercy and hear my prayer, for I trust in You. Have mercy on me, who am full of sin and sorrow, for the depth of Your compassion has no end. Praise to You, O saving sacrifice, offered on the wood of the cross for me and for all mankind! Praise to the noble and precious Blood, flowing from the wounds of my crucified Lord Jesus Christ and washing away the sins of the whole world! Remember, O Lord, Your creation, which You have redeemed by Your Blood. I repent of my sins, and I long to put right what I have done wrong. O Merciful Father, take away all my offenses and sins; purify me in body and soul, and make me worthy to taste the Holy of Holies. May Your Body and Blood, which I intend to receive, though I am unworthy, be for the remission of my sins, the washing away of my guilt, the end of my evil thoughts, and the rebirth of my better instincts. May it incite me to do the works that are pleasing to You and beneficial to both my soul and body, and let it be a firm defense against the wiles of my enemies.

PRAYERS OF ST. AUGUSTINE OF HIPPO

TO THE HOLY SPIRIT

 REATHE IN ME, O Holy Spirit, that my thoughts may all be holy.

Act in me, O Holy Spirit, that my work, too, may
  be holy.

Draw my heart, O Holy Spirit, that I love but what
  is holy.

Strengthen me, O Holy Spirit, to defend all that is holy.

Guard me, then, O Holy Spirit, that I may always
  be holy.

A Prayer for the Indwelling of the Holy Spirit

 Holy Spirit, powerful Consoler, sacred bond of the Father and the Son, hope of the afflicted, descend into my heart and establish therein Your loving dominion. Kindle the fire of Your love in my tepid soul, so that I may be wholly obedient to You. We believe that when You dwell in us, You also prepare a dwelling for the Father and the Son. Therefore deign to come to me, O Comforter of the forlorn and Advocate of the needy. Help the afflicted, strengthen the weak, and support the wavering. Come and purify me, and let no evil desire take possession of me. You love the humble and resist the proud. Come to me, O glory of the living and hope of the dying. Lead me by Your grace that I may always be pleasing to You. Amen.

A Prayer for the Afflicted

Watch, O Lord, with those who wake, or watch, or weep tonight, and give Your angels charge over those who sleep. Tend Your sick ones, O Lord Christ. Rest Your weary ones. Bless Your dying ones. Soothe Your suffering ones. Pity Your afflicted

ones. Shield Your joyous ones. And all for the sake of
Your love. Amen.

A Prayer for Self-Knowledge

 Lord Jesus, let me know myself and You,
and desire nothing save only You.

Let me hate myself and love You.

Let me do everything for the sake of You.

Let me humble myself and exalt You.

Let me think of nothing except You.

Let me die to myself and live in You.

Let me accept whatever happens as from You.

Let me banish myself and follow You, and ever desire to
follow You.

Let me flee from myself and take refuge in You,

That I may deserve to be defended by You.

Let me fear for myself.

Let me fear You, and let me be among those who are
chosen by You.

Let me distrust myself and put my trust in You.

Let me be willing to obey for the sake of You.

Let me cling to nothing but You,

And let me be poor because of You.

Look upon me, that I may love You.

Beckon me that I may see You and forever rejoice in
    You. Amen.

A Prayer of Hope

For Your mercy's sake, O Lord my God,
tell me what You are to me. Say to my soul, "I am
your salvation." So speak that I may hear, O Lord; my
heart is listening; open it that it may hear You, and say to
my soul, "I am your salvation." After hearing this word,
may I come in haste to take hold of You. Hide not Your
face from me. Let me behold Your face even if I die, lest
I die with longing to see it. The house of my soul is too
small to receive You; let it be enlarged by You. It is all
in ruins; do You repair it. There are things in it—I confess and I know—that must offend Your sight. But who
shall cleanse it? Or to whom besides You shall I cry out?
From my secret sins cleanse me, O Lord, and from those
of others spare Your servant. Amen.

You Are Christ

ou are Christ,
my Holy Father,

my Tender God,

my Great King,

my Good Shepherd,

my Only Master,

my Best Helper,

my Most Beautiful and my Beloved,

my Living Bread,

my Priest Forever,

my Country's Leader,

my True Light,

my Holy Sweetness,

my Straight Path,

my Supreme Wisdom,

my Pure Simplicity,

my Peaceful Harmony,

my Complete Protection,

my Good Portion,

my Everlasting Salvation.

The Breastplate of
St. Patrick of Ireland

I ARISE TODAY
Through a mighty strength, the invocation
   of the Trinity,
Through belief in the Threeness,
Through confession of the Oneness of the Creator
   of creation.

I ARISE TODAY
Through the strength of Christ's Birth and His Baptism,
Through the strength of His Crucifixion and His Burial,
Through the strength of His Resurrection and His
   Ascension,
Through the strength of His descent for the judgment
   of doom.

I ARISE TODAY
Through the strength of the love of the cherubim,
In the obedience of angels,
In the service of archangels,
In the hope of resurrection to meet with reward,

In the prayers of patriarchs,

In the predictions of prophets,

In the preaching of apostles,

In the faith of confessors,

In the innocence of holy virgins,

In the deeds of righteous men.

I ARISE TODAY,

Through the strength of heaven,

The light of the sun,

The radiance of the moon,

The splendor of fire,

The speed of lightning,

The swiftness of wind,

The depth of the sea,

The stability of the earth,

The firmness of the rocks.

I ARISE TODAY,

Through God's strength to lead me,

God's might to uphold me,

God's wisdom to guide me,

God's eye to look before me,

God's ear to hear me,

God's word to speak for me,

God's hand to guard me,

God's shield to protect me,

God's host to save me

From the snares of devils,

From the temptation of vices,

From everyone who shall wish me ill, afar and near.

I SUMMON TODAY

All these powers between me and those evils,

Against every cruel and merciless power that may oppose
  my soul and body,

Against the incantations of false prophets,

Against the dark laws of heathenism,

Against the false laws of heretics,

Against the craft of idolatry,

Against the spells of witches, conjurers, and augurers,

Against every knowledge that corrupts man's body
  and soul;

Christ to shield me today

Against poison, against burning,

Against drowning, against wounding,

So that there may come to me an abundance of reward.

Christ with me,

Christ before me,

Christ behind me,

Christ in me,

Christ beneath me,

Christ above me,

Christ on my right,

Christ on my left,

Christ when I lie down,

Christ when I sit down,

Christ when I rise,

Christ in the heart of all who think of me,

Christ in the mouth of all who speak of me,

Christ in every eye that sees me,

Christ in every ear that hears me.

Prayer of St. Dimitri of Rostov

 PEN, O DOORS and bolts of my heart, that
Christ the King of Glory may enter!

Enter, O my Light, and enlighten my darkness;

Enter, O my Life, and quicken my deadness;

Enter, O my Physician, and heal my wounds;

Enter, O Divine Fire, and burn up the thorns of my sins;

Ignite my inward parts and my heart with the flame of
   Your love;

Enter, O my King, and destroy in me the kingdom
   of sin;

Sit on the throne of my heart and alone reign in me,
   O my King and my Lord!

Prayers of St. Gregory of Nyssa

Of God's Goodness

Lord, from You flows true and continual kindness. You had cast us off, and justly so, but in Your
mercy You forgave us. You were at odds with us, and
You reconciled us. You had laid a curse on us, and You
blessed us. You had banished us from the garden, and
You called us back again. You took away the fig leaves
that had been an unsuitable garment, and You clothed us
in a cloak of great value. You flung wide the prison gates,
and You pardoned the condemned. You sprinkled clean
water on us, and You washed away the dirt.

To the Good Shepherd

Where are You pasturing Your flock, O Good Shepherd, who carry the whole flock on Your shoulders? For the whole of human nature is one sheep, and You have lifted it upon Your shoulders. Show me the place of peace, lead me to the good pasture that will nourish me, call me by name so that I, Your sheep, may hear Your voice, and by Your speech give me eternal life. Answer me, You whom my soul loves.

I give You the name "You whom my soul loves" because Your name is above every name and above all understanding, and there is no rational nature that can utter it or comprehend it. Therefore Your name, by which Your goodness is known, is simply the love my soul has for You. How could I not love You, when You loved me so much, even though my heart was black, that You laid down Your life for the sheep of Your flock? A greater love cannot be imagined than exchanging Your life for my salvation.

Show me then (says my soul) where You pasture Your flock, so that I can find that saving pasture too, and fill myself with the food of heaven without which no one can come to eternal life, and run to the spring and fill myself with the drink of God. You give it, as from a spring, to those who thirst—water pouring from Your side cut open by the lance, water that, to whoever drinks it, is a fountain of water springing up to eternal life.

If You lead me to pasture here, You will make me lie down at noon, sleeping at peace and taking my rest in light unstained by any shade. For the noon has no shade and the sun stands far above the mountain peaks. You bring Your flock to lie in this light when You bring Your children to rest with You in Your bed. But no one can be judged worthy of this noonday rest who is not a child of light and a child of the day. Whoever has separated himself equally from the shadows of evening and morning, from where evil begins and evil ends, at noon he will lie down and the sun of righteousness will shine on him.

Show me, then (says my soul), how I should sleep and how I should graze, and where the path is to my noonday rest. Do not let me fall away from Your flock because of ignorance and find myself one of a flock of sheep that are not Yours.

Thus spoke my soul, when she was anxious about the beauty that God's care had given her and wanted to know how she could keep this good fortune forever.

Prayers of St. Gregory the Theologian

To the All-Transcendent God

 ALL-TRANSCENDENT GOD (and what other name could describe You?), what words can sing Your praises? No word does You justice. What mind can probe Your secrets? No mind can encompass You. You alone are beyond the power of speech, yet all that we speak stems from You. You alone are beyond the power of thought, yet all that we can conceive springs from You. All things proclaim You, those endowed with reason and those bereft of it. All the expectation and pain of the world coalesces in You. All things utter a prayer to You, a silent hymn composed by You. You sustain everything that exists, and all things move together at Your command. You are the goal of all that exists. You are one and You are all, yet You are none of the things that exist, neither a part nor the whole. You can avail Yourself of any name; how shall I call You, the only unnamable? All-transcendent God!

A Prayer for the Dead
and for Preparing for Death

 Lord and Creator of all, and especially of Your creature, man: You are the God and Father and ruler of Your children; You are the Lord of life and death; You are the guardian and benefactor of our souls. You fashion and transform all things in their due season through Your creating Word, as You know to be best in Your deep wisdom and providence. Receive now those who have gone ahead of us in our journey from this life. Receive us too at the proper time, when You have guided us in our bodily life as long as may be for our profit. Receive us prepared indeed by fear of You, but not troubled, not shrinking back on that day of death or uprooted by force like those who are lovers of the world and the flesh. Instead, may we set out eagerly for that everlasting and blessed life which is in Christ Jesus our Lord, to whom be glory forever and ever. Amen.

Prayers of St. John Chrysostom for Every Hour of the Day

12:00 A.M.

O Lord, You know Your creation and what You have willed for it; let Your will also be fulfilled in me, a sinner. For blessed are You forevermore.

1:00 A.M.

O Lord, deprive me not of Your heavenly blessings.

2:00 A.M.

O Lord, deliver me from eternal torment.

3:00 A.M.

O Lord, if I have sinned in my will or thought, in word or deed, forgive me.

4:00 A.M.

O Lord, deliver me from all ignorance and heedlessness, from pettiness of the soul and hardness of heart.

5:00 A.M.

O Lord, deliver me from every temptation.

6:00 A.M.

O Lord, enlighten my heart darkened by evil desires.

7:00 A.M.

I, BEING HUMAN, have sinned, O Lord; do You, being God, forgive me in Your lovingkindness, for You know the weakness of my soul.

8:00 A.M.

O Lord, send down Your grace to help me, that I may glorify Your holy name.

9:00 A.M.

O Lord Jesus Christ, inscribe my name in the Book of Life, and grant me, Your servant, a blessed end.

10:00 A.M.

O Lord my God, even if I have done nothing good in Your sight, yet grant that, by Your grace, I may make a beginning of doing good.

11:00 A.M.

O Lord, sprinkle upon my heart the dew of Your grace.

12:00 P.M.

O LORD of heaven and earth, remember me, Your sinful servant, who am cold of heart and impure, in Your Kingdom.

1:00 P.M.

O LORD, receive my repentance.

2:00 P.M.

O LORD, do not forsake me.

3:00 P.M.

O LORD, save me from temptation.

4:00 P.M.

O LORD, grant me pure thoughts.

5:00 P.M.

O LORD, grant me tears of repentance, remembrance of death, and the sense of peace.

6:00 P.M.

O Lord, grant me mindfulness to confess my sins.

7:00 P.M.

O Lord, grant me humility, charity, and obedience.

8:00 P.M.

O Lord, grant me long-suffering, charity, and meekness.

9:00 P.M.

O Lord, implant in me the root of all blessings: the fear of You in my heart.

10:00 P.M.

O Lord, grant that I may love You with all my heart and soul, and that I may obey Your will in all things.

11:00 P.M.

O Lord, shield me from wicked men, from demons and passions, and from all other ungodly things.

Prayer at Daybreak by Elder Sophrony of Essex

E<small>TERNAL</small> K<small>ING</small>, You are without beginning; You were there before the worlds were made. You are my Maker, who summoned all things from non-being into life. Bless this day which You, in Your ineffable goodness, have given to me. By the power of Your blessing, enable me at all times in this coming day to speak and act for You, for Your glory, in Your fear, according to Your will, with a pure spirit, and with humility, patience, love, gentleness, peace, courage, wisdom, and prayer, aware of Your presence in all places.

Yes, O Lord, in Your bountiful mercy, lead me by Your Holy Spirit to every good work and word, and grant me to walk in Your sight without stumbling all the days of my life, according to Your righteousness that You have revealed to us, that I may not add to my transgressions.

O Lord, great in mercy, spare me, for I perish in wickedness; hide not Your face from me. And when my perverted will would lead me down other paths, do not forsake me, O my Savior, but bring me back to Your holy path.

O Good One, to whom all hearts are open, You know my poverty and my foolishness, my blindness and my uselessness, but the afflictions of my soul are also laid before You. Therefore I beseech You: Hear me in my affliction and fill me with Your strength from above. Raise me up, who am paralyzed with sin, and deliver me, who am enslaved to the passions. Heal me of every hidden wound. Purify me of all defilement of flesh and spirit. Preserve me from every inward and outward impulse that is unpleasing in Your sight and hurtful to my neighbor.

I beseech You: Establish me in the path of Your commandments, and until my last breath let me not stray from the light of Your ordinances, so that Your commandments may become the sole law of my being in this life and in the eternal life to come.

O God, my God, I plead with You for many and great things: do not disregard me. Cast me not away from Your presence because of my presumption and boldness, but by the power of Your love, lead me in the path of Your will. Grant me to love You as You have commanded, with all my heart, and with all my soul, and with all my mind, and with all my strength: with my whole being.

For You alone are the holy guardian and all-powerful defender of my life, and to You I offer prayer and glory.

Before I depart from this life, grant me the knowledge of Your truth. Preserve my life in this world until I offer You true repentance. Do not take me away in the midst of my days, and when You are pleased to bring my life to an end, forewarn me of my death, that I may prepare my soul to come before You.

Be with me then, O Lord, on that great and sacred day, and grant me the joy of Your salvation. Cleanse me from my sins, manifest and hidden, from all iniquity concealed within me; and grant me a good defense before Your dread judgment seat. AMEN.

EXTRACTS FROM PRAYERS BY THE LAKE BY ST. NIKOLAI VELIMIROVIC

NOINT MY HEART with the oil of Your mercy, my most merciful Lord.

May neither anger against the strong nor contempt for the weak ever erupt in my heart! For all things are frailer than the morning dew.

May hatred never make a nest in my heart against those who plot evil against me, so that I may be mindful of their end and be at peace.

Mercifulness opens the way to the heart of all creatures and brings joy. Mercilessness brings fog to the fore and creates a confined isolation.

Have mercy on Your merciful servant, O most Tender Hand, and reveal to me the mystery of Your mercy.

O MY LOVE, would that I could motivate all the inhabitants of the earth, waters, and sky to sing a hymn to You! Would that I could remove leprosy from the face of the earth and turn this wanton world back into the sort of virgin that You created!

Truly, my God, You are just as great with or without the world.

You are equally great whether the world glorifies You or whether the world blasphemes You. But when the world blasphemes You, You seem even greater in the eyes of Your saints.

O Lord, my dream day and night, help me to magnify You, so that nothing may become great in my heart except You.

Let all creatures magnify You, O Lord, lest they make themselves great instead of You.

Truly, You are exceedingly great, O Lord; would that all our hymns could make You greater!

Lord, O Lord, do not scorch us with Your radiance, which is unbearable for our eyes; and do not leave us in the gloom where one grows old and decays. You alone know the measure of our needs. O Lord, glory to You!

O my Lord, make haste to show a new way to every penitent after he scorns his old way.

O heavenly Mother, Bride of the All-Holy Spirit, bow down toward our heart when we repent. Open the fountain of tears within us, that we may wash away the heavy clay that saddens our eyes.

O All-Holy Spirit, blow away and disperse the unclean stench from the soul of the penitent that has been choking him, and lead him to repentance.

We bow down and beseech You, O Life-giving and Mighty Spirit!

FOR ALL THE SINS of men I repent before You, O Most Merciful Lord. Indeed, the seed of all sins flows in my blood! With my effort and Your mercy I choke this wicked crop of weeds day and night, so that no tare may sprout in the field of the Lord, but only pure wheat.

I repent for all those who are worried, who stagger under a burden of anxieties and do not know that they should cast all their troubles on You. For feeble man, even the most minor worry is unbearable, but for You a mountain of worries is like a snowball thrown into a fiery furnace.

I repent for all the sick, for sickness is the fruit of sin. When the soul is cleansed with repentance, sickness disappears with sin, and You, my Eternal Health, take up Your abode in the soul.

I repent for unbelievers, who through their unbelief amass worries and sicknesses both on themselves and on their friends.

I repent for all those who blaspheme God, who blaspheme against You without knowing that they are blaspheming against the Master, who clothes them and feeds them.

I repent for all the slayers of men, who take the life of another to preserve their own. Forgive them, Most Merciful Lord, for they know not what they do. For they do not know that there are not two lives in the universe, but one, and that there are not two men in the universe, but one. O how dead are those who cut the heart in half!

I repent for all those who bear false witness, for in reality they are homicides and suicides.

For all my brothers who are thieves and who are hoarders of unneeded wealth, I weep and sigh, for they have buried their soul and have nothing with which to go forth before You.

For all the arrogant and the boastful I weep and sigh, for before You they are like beggars with empty pockets.

For all drunkards and gluttons I weep and sigh, for they have become servants of their servants.

For all adulterers I repent, for they have betrayed the trust of the Holy Spirit, who chose them to form new life through them. Instead, they turned serving life into destroying life.

For all gossipers I repent, for they have turned Your most precious gift, the gift of speech, into cheap sand.

For all those who destroy their neighbor's hearth and home and their neighbor's peace I repent and sigh, for they bring a curse on themselves and their people.

For all lying tongues, for all suspicious eyes, for all raging hearts, for all insatiable stomachs, for all darkened minds, for all ill will, for all unseemly thoughts, for all murderous emotions—I repent, weep, and sigh.

For all the history of mankind from Adam to me, a sinner, I repent; for all history is in my blood. For I am in Adam and Adam is in me.

For all the worlds, large and small, that do not tremble before Your awesome presence, I weep and cry out:
O Master Most Merciful, have mercy on me and save me!

Calendar of the Great Feasts and Fasts of the Church

The Twelve Great Feasts

*Dates are given in Gregorian
followed by Julian calendar.*

Fixed Feasts
The Theophany of Our Lord
January 6/19

The Meeting of the Lord
February 2/15

The Annunciation to the Theotokos
March 25/April 7

The Transfiguration of Our Lord
August 6/19

The Dormition of the Mother of God
August 15/28

The Nativity of the Mother of God
September 8/21

The Exaltation of the Cross
September 14/27

The Entry of the Mother of God
November 21/December 4

The Nativity of Our Lord
December 25/January 7

MOVABLE FEASTS
(depending on the date of Pascha)

Palm Sunday	*The Sunday before Pascha*
Ascension Thursday	*Forty days after Pascha*
Pentecost Sunday	*Fifty days after Pascha*

THE FASTS
Great Lent and Holy Week (7 weeks)
Clean Monday to Pascha

The Apostles' Fast (variable length)
Monday after All Saints' Day (Sunday after Pentecost)
until the eve of the Feast of Ss. Peter and Paul
June 29/July 12

The Dormition Fast (2 weeks)
      August 1–14/14–27

Advent (40 days)
      November 15–December 24/
      November 28–January 6

Individual Fasting Days

The Eve of the Theophany
      January 5/18

The Beheading of St. John the Baptist
      August 29/September 11

The Great Feast of the Exaltation of the Cross
      September 14/27

Wednesdays and Fridays apart from:
The week following the Sunday of the
Publican and the Pharisee (*the third week before Great Lent*)

Trinity Week (*the week after Pentecost*)

Christmastide
      December 25–January 4/January 7–19

Variation:
Renewal Week *(the week after Pascha)*
or
all of Eastertide *(Pascha–Ascension)*

Fasting from meat only:
Cheese Week *(the week before Great Lent)*

Fish is permitted on Wednesdays and Fridays when they coincide with one of the Great Feasts *(except for the Feast of the Exaltation of the Cross).*

DATES OF ORTHODOX PASCHA
AND LATIN EASTER

	ORTHODOX PASCHA	LATIN EASTER
2015	April 12	April 5
2016	May 1	March 27
2017	April 16	April 16
2018	April 8	April 1
2019	April 28	April 21
2020	April 19	April 12
2021	May 2	April 4
2022	April 24	April 17
2023	April 16	April 9
2024	May 5	March 31
2025	April 20	April 20

PRAYERS FOR THE LIVING

PRAYERS FOR THE LIVING

PRAYERS FOR THE DEPARTED

PRAYERS FOR THE DEPARTED